# Early Anti-British Revolts in Andhra; 1766-1857

# Early Anti-British Revolts in Andhra; 1766-1857

**Professor K.S.S. Seshan**

GYAN

First Published, 2018

*Published by*

Gyan Publishing House
5, Ansari Road
Daryaganj, New Delhi-110002
Phone: 9811692060
E-mail: books@gyanbooks.com

*Printed at:* G. Print Process, Delhi.

**Cataloging in Publication Data—DK**
Courtesy: D.K. Agencies (P) Ltd. <docinfo@dkagencies.com>

**Seshan, K. S. S.,** 1941- **author.**
Early anti-British revolts in Andhra, 1766-1857 / Professor K.S.S. Seshan.
pages cm
Includes bibliographical references.
ISBN 9788121214292

1. Revolutions—India—Andhra Pradesh—History—18th century.
2. Revolutions—India—Andhra Pradesh—History—19th century.
3. Andhra Pradesh (India)—Politics and government—18th century.
4. Andhra Pradesh (India)—Politics and government—19th century.
5. India—History—British occupation, 1765-1947. I. Title.

LCC DS485.A555S47 2018 | DDC 954.85031 23

For

my grandchildren: Makarand, Sai Juhitha and Bhargav; with the hope that when they grow up, this will ignite their interest to delve deep into the way our nation stood up against colonialism, for the cause of which, Early Revolts of this kind all over the country, were of consequence.

# Contents

# Foreword

Perhaps no questions have so beset historians of India, or political thinkers, as those relating the structural stability of political systems. The larger the political structure, the more acute and persistent the concern. The larger a political system, the more it has been afflicted by structural instability; moreover, the larger the structure, the more problematic its longevity.

The survival of political systems depended not only upon how much political wisdom could inform decisions but also on how long support from local forces could be held. Failures could spell ruin. Failures could also bring serious repercussions. Conversely, the smaller were political entities, the more long lasting was their stability, durability, and antiquity. Some high-born and elite family lineages traced themselves back many centuries. Some middle-sized political entities that last for generations. Where scores of elite communities co-existed, however uneasily, within multi-ethnic and multi-cultural contexts, each claiming distinct ritual purity and status better than the other, where marriage alliances between different lineages were the exception rather than the rule, common grounds for sharing a political commonwealth of authority or legitimacy became difficult to achieve. Under such circumstances, where micro-ethnicities and micro-polities co-existed, like molecules within a colloidal suspension, it was difficult to bring together many "small hard pieces" so as to erect larger and more durable political structures. Dialectical tensions of material, social, and ritual distance were too great, too difficult to transcend. Larger structures tended to break down into more elemental pieces — like rust corroding iron. An inverse ration existed between size and durability. No larger "state" could last without its inner structures being riddled undermined by smaller "anti-bodies" in different kinds. Rebellions and subversions were symptomatic of more basic and elemental loyalties. Force, and only force, had limitations. The dictums set forth by Benoy Kumar Sarkar, namely, that "a sword-less state is a contradiction in terms" can be countered by Lord Acton, that "power corrupts and absolute power corrupts absolutely". Larger, more powerful structures become corrupted. Parasitic microbes, many too small to catch, eat away inner structures state like so many white ants eating away a piece of furniture from within. Larger structure scrambling from within when assaulted. Like passing phenomena, they could be like illusions (reflecting cosmic *maya*).

The peculiar fragility of structures of 'higher authority' in India, so vexing in political history and theory, has been a feature which, at its deepest levels, can be perceived a rising out of differing cultural, ethical, and religious convictions about essentials, about the nature of reality and, consequently, about the limits of demands which might be made upon persons holding differing convictions. The degree to which any single kind of "rule of law" was possible, for holding political systems together, could only reach so far. A legal structure could never reach beyond certain limits – of communal and personal agreements, or bonds or contracts, as embodied and institutionalized within segmented social structures: bonds of local custom (embodied and reinforced by sacred norms, domestic and cosmic) which held each ethnic community together.

Relationships between conflicting ethical systems and processes of structural integration within the segmented societies of India can hardly be understood without how the limits of loyalty were violated. Over and over again, instances of ideological and institutional imposition brought fresh conflicts between client and patron, between subordinates and superiors, between contract holders whose bonds of fealty were being violated. Tensions over social distinction, over social distance, over social or ritual purity, and over social and sacred space can be seen as a recurring theme in documents and records. Reports from various localities told much the same story. Local sources, especially relating to bonds of administrative, military and political service – as reflected in land grants, bureaucratic appointments, military titles, or religious endowments – are replete with details of murky controversy. Stresses came from increasingly radical and rapid pace of change occurring within the political culture, from changes which threatened to restructure social realities.

More specifically, what stretched local loyalties beyond tolerance can be found in instances of locally perceived grievances. Any 'wrongful' action was one which violated bonds of contract (*namak-halal*), and of an incredible variety. Any violation of social custom or ritual purity which was held to be sacred, especially if its implications might be seen by some constituent elements within the Raj as having cosmic or divine significance, could bring about dire political consequences and could shake the foundations of political stability in a locality. Any change in usage, whether of buildings, conveyances, drinking water, food, garments, hostels (*chattirams*), roads, schools, temples, or facilities of any other kind, not excluding forms of involuntary servitude, such as pulling temple cars (not to mention temple rituals), could quickly transgress the limits of loyalty and put the larger political structures into jeopardy.

Heedless officials and policy makers, especially those ignorant about the nature of social and religious constraints in local traditions, often found it convenient to gloss over such events. They often failed to explain or sometimes did not bother to find out what might actually have happened. Words like 'spontaneous' or 'unexpected' used to describe causes for local unrest about in local records. There is an abundance of evidence pertaining to various different categories of conflict which served to demonstrate how the outer religious and socio-ethical limits of any form of state 'secularity' were, in some way, transgressed.

Historical events within Telugu country, as astutely shown within pages of local history given us by Professor K. S. S. Seshan, reflect such axioms as those mentioned above. Each encounter of the Company's Raj with different local entities as "small hard pieces" or "little kingdoms", and with their different cultural particularities, presented fresh and unforeseen challenges. Each expansion of the imperial system altered the nature of the Raj itself. Verities of political understanding were moulded and remoulded, often transgressing what local people were able to appreciate and comprehend. Each local people held its own perceptions of primal verity. Elemental impulses within human experience – each in a time or place – reflected underlying primal essentials. Each local people struggled against new and radical superimpositions of larger and more powerful state-imposed institutions. Whatever was being "transformed" as each encounter sank deeper and deeper into local cultural soil, brought resistance. Each encounter brought specific responses, either of acceptance, rejection, or resistance. New ceremonials, creeds and doctrines, institutions and ideals, as well as qualities and styles of life reflected fresh forms of verity. Thus, just as the human body as a structural whole deploys antibodies to combat alien and virulent antigen, so localities reacted to perceived alien and predatory forces that were perceived as threatening.

It is just such localizing features of traditional processes of power within the history of Telugu country during the rule of the East India Company that Professor Seshan has explored so relentlessly in the work which this Foreword addresses. In so doing, he has followed an historiographical path opened over sixty years ago with publication of my *Guntur District, 1788-1848: A History of Local Influence and Central Authority in South India* (Oxford: 1965). This path has been widened further with the recent publication of *A Muslim Conspiracy in British India: Politics and Paranoia in the Early Nineteenth Century Deccan* (Cambridge: 2017), by Professor Chandra Sekhar Mallampalli. It is, therefore, a pleasure to extol the publication of yet another work that delves into the intricacies of rebellion, resistance, and subversion of larger political structures being forged, if fitfully, by the statecraft of the East India Company's construction of that Raj that would eventually evolve into what would become the modern India of our day. Fresh research such as this challenges our historical understandings.

**Robert Eric Frykenberg**

University of Wisconsin –
Madison (U.S.A.)

# Preface

The nationwide Sesquicentennial celebrations of the Great Revolt of 1857 a decade ago, has evoked an unprecedented interest not only on the First War of Independence, but also on the nature and content of the revolts that occurred prior to it. The revolts, though sporadic and were on a smaller scale during the century preceding 1857, are of significance as they not only provided inspiration but also specified the direction and ideological background for the later major revolts. They were like the nurseries out of which the anti-British sentiments grew into revolts and eventually snowballed into the struggle for freedom.

The present study, "Early Anti- British Revolts in Andhra, 1766-1857" deals with such Pre-1857 revolts in Seemandhra (Rayalaseema and Coastal Andhra) region of Andhra Pradesh. As the erstwhile State of Hyderabad was under the Nizam's rule, the rebellions in Telangana area form beyond the scope of this study. However, the Bolaram Mutiny of 1855 is studied for the significant role it played on the eve of the 1857 Revolt which was nationwide. Ganjam, (along with Gajapathi District) which at present is in Orissa State, is included in this study for it was an integral part of the then Northern Circars. The period chosen for the study is between 1766 when the Circars were first acquired by the British and 1857 when the Great Revolt broke leading to the end of the Company administration.

The Anti-British Revolts of the Zamindars in the Circars and the Palegars' Revolts in the Ceded Districts and in the Chittoor areas are taken for this study. Though some of the Anti- British Revolts fought by the Raja of Vizianagaram and the revolt of Uyyalawada Narasimha Reddy (1846) are popularly known, many others like the Thornekal Rebellion, the Chittoor Palegars' Revolt, the Wahabi Conspiracy of the Nawab of Kurnool and the Mutiny at Bolaram (1855) etc .are hardly known. An attempt is made in this study to assess the nature, content and consequences of the revolts with a historical perspective.

For the present study, apart from consulting the archival sources preserved in the governmental repositories, private individual collections at various places, and oral sources through field-study are given importance. The oral testimonies on the revolts in their region provide interesting facets to the historical occurrences. Even at this distance of time, those heroic movements continue to live in the collective memory, transcending the *long dure* as a legacy in the form of legends and myths and in myriad folk forms. Though the oral testimonies are no substitute to recorded evidences, they amply testify the extent to which the revolts and those involved in such revolts have impacted the imagination of the successive generations. However, care has been taken to check the veracity of such oral testimonies with documentary evidences.

The revolts in Andhra against the British were motivated with the desire to drive away the foreign masters. These revolts were inherently due to the opposition of the Zamindars and the Palegars who earlier were accustomed to enjoy uninterrupted powers during the successive dynasties. Though the chiefs knew that the British Company forces were better equipped, better armed with modern weapons, the strong conviction that "*they* (the British army men in India) *are few and we are many*", largely motivated them to take to rebellions. Though these revolts did not achieve the objectives for which they were started, they did help in instilling the spirit of anti - British sentiment among the people. The spread of such a feeling and the sacrifices the Zamindars and other chiefs made, though sporadic in nature, took the overall struggle against colonialism to greater heights.

**K.S.S. Seshan**

# Acknowledgements

The present book, *EARLY ANTI- BRITISH REVOLTS IN ANDHRA, 1766-1857* would not have been possible without a research grant from the Indian Council of Historical Studies, (ICHR) New Delhi. A visit to the British Library, London, for consulting source materials and visits to the Universities of Glasgow and Edinburgh in search of Family Papers and the Archival materials on the life and work of Thomas Munro, and a visit to Bodleian Library, Oxford, were all made possible by a foreign travel grant from the ICHR. I thank the ICHR for the above grants. I thank Mr. Manoj Bejjani of Sainsbury, for the engaging academic discussions and the scholarly company he provided while in London, to consult records at the British Library.

I thank the Vice-Chancellor, the Registrar and the Department of History, University of Hyderabad, for the Institutional affiliation extended to me for carrying out the research project.

I thank Prof. Simon Charsley of the University of Glasgow, Dr. Sridhar Modugu, Fellow at the University of Edinburgh and Prof. Barbara Harris-White, of Oxford University, for making my visits to those Universities more fruitful and academically stimulating.

I profusely thank Prof. Robert E. Frykenberg of the University of Wisconsin, Madison, a trend setter in the field of Historical research in Modern Andhra, for his constant encouragement and for the very generous Foreword, he wrote for the book.

My thanks are due to the Director and staff of the Andhra Pradesh State Archives, Hyderabad and the Librarian, University of Hyderabad for the help they extended. I thank Mr. M. Rajender Reddy who, as Research Assistant of the project, assiduously extended every possible help. I also thank my colleagues in the Department, Prof. K.P. Rao and Dr. M.N. Rajesh who have been helpful throughout the period of the study. I thank Dr. Murali Manohar of the Centre for Human Rights, University of Hyderabad, for all the help he rendered. My thanks are also due to my daughter, Ms. Shatpada, for her incisive insights, diligent scrutiny and critical observations on several Chapters of this book.

I thank Messrs. Paramesh, Subramanyam, and Ravi for the secretarial assistance they extended.

My thanks are due to Mr. Amit Garg, the Director and his very able staff at Gyan Publishing House, New Delhi, for bringing out the book in its present elegant form, in such a short span.

**K.S.S. Seshan**

December, 2017

# Chapter - 1

# Introduction

Opposition to British rule in India began almost from the very establishment of their rule. The nature of the British rule was such that it invited protest movements in several parts of the country. The 1857 rebellion was preceded by a wave of uprisings in the late eighteenth and first half of the nineteenth centuries. The thrust of these uprisings was to contest the nature of changes that were brought about by the East India Company in the country. The Company's administration tried to re-order an existing feudal order to ensure the political and economic stability of the empire. This process led to a severe discontent among the traditional land holders and the peasantry comprising of the cultivators and tenant farmers, tribals and even landless labourers who were dependent on agriculture and its allied sectors for their livelihood.[1]

The primary reason for such an opposition to the British was the anti- people agenda of the colonial administration. Several native rulers were dethroned, their kingdoms occupied; the Zamindars and Palegars were removed and their lands sequestrated; the traditional arts and crafts were ruined as they were overpowered by the import of machine made goods of the west; *Inams*, the age old privileged land tenures were abolished much to the annoyance of the local landed gentry; Kattubadies, the conventional local constabulary was replaced with a new system of Police that threw into disarray the entire rural elite on to the offensive. The innovative revenue collecting measures, with systems like the Zamindari, Ryotwari, Mahalwari, Malguzari, Visabadi and the like, only distanced the peasants and land holders from the gambit of the administration. Almost every branch in society and economy was hit by the colonial rule.

British colonialism did not remain uniform from the beginning to the end of their rule. It underwent several phases depending on the economic needs of the mother country. As Bipan Chandra has ably argued, the Indian economy was subordinated to the British economy and Indian administration was tuned to their economic needs.[2] In the initial decades of the British rule, monopoly of trade and appropriation of land revenue was the dominant factor that marked their rule. This was to be followed by exploitation through trade, and in later phases, there was also exploitation through foreign investment and international competition for colonies. But whatever was the colonial phase, appropriation of surplus continued unabated during the entire period of their rule.[3]

Land was transformed into a state property and the old bonds of economic cooperation with common interests among the villagers was erased.[4] Land rent was given utmost importance in their administrative priorities. Heavy tributes were collected from the subordinate rulers, Chiefs and revenue farmers as a result of which, the peasants had to bear the brunt of heavy taxation. The Company transformed itself into the supreme 'Land-lord' in India. The normal dictum for the Company officials in India from the Home government has been ' maximum revenue with minimum expenditure'. The rural population was the worst hit due to such land revenue policies. They collected land rents as a rule, in cash. Madras Presidency when compared to Bengal and Bombay, was the most heavily taxed residency.[5] Several of their prerogatives were taken away. In case of failure of payments on time, there was the inevitable risk of loosing the lands.

There was also discontentment among the tribals. Their rights and privileges were trampled by the avaricious alien rulers. Forest wealth to which the tribals had unlimited access was monopolized by the Company administration through curbs on the traditional rights of the tribal populations to food, fuel and fodder in the forests. The colonial state was also responsible for the influx of money lenders, Mahajans and merchants to disrupt the autonomy of the tribals. Such middlemen also were responsible to bring the tribals into the vortex of colonial economy and exploitation. [6] The British rule and its commercialization process ended the self sufficient economy of the tribals and brought them within the fold of colonialism. As a result, the revolts and rebellions during the period prior to 1857, were mostly propelled by the dispossessed Zamindars, Palegars, and their 'reliable allies'- peasants, tribals and even weavers. Artisans were prominent in the riots in several parts of the country. For example, in Rohilkhand and Benares they rose in revolt between 1809 and 1818. Weavers' protests were widespread in Visakhapatnam and Godavari Districts in Andhra.[7]

In the beginning, the opposition to the British rule took the nature of self sacrificing sporadic Peasant revolts. The simmering discontent burst into acts of open defiance and some times of violence in several parts of the country. Most frequently the Zamindars and other local chiefs fought enhancement of rent, evictions, confiscation of lands and abolition of their traditional privileges. [8]

Apart from the land revenue policies of the British, there were also other reasons for incurring the wrath of the local chiefs, the Zamindars and the peasants. The Company servants, at least many of them, were new to administration. Their thrust was on trade and commerce. They were ignorant of the local customs, socio-economic conditions and the traditional land relations. Ignorance of such indigenous conditions coupled with the avaricious desire to make big profits, made the Company servants to resort to maximum collections; and collecting to the last pie, regardless of the existing conditions.

## Centers of Early Revolts

There were broadly three or four distinct processes that led to the uprisings between 1757 and 1857. The most important one as stated earlier, was the nature of the land settlement process which structured all British policies throughout this period. The conquest of Bengal led to the Permanent Settlement, while Ryotwari settlements were introduced in Madras Presidency, Mahalwari tenures in the North and Malguzari in several parts of Central India.

The British promulgated rules where the lands of the revenue defaulters could be auctioned to a new class of land holders. This meant that the traditional land holders like the Zamindars and Palegars were converted from people who governed and administered their estates to mere revenue collectors and farmers. This created a disgruntled class of displaced Zamindars who provided leadership to many protests of the period either themselves or through their military. It is interesting to note that some of the most representative rebellions of the traditional chiefs and revenue collectors who lost their powers because of colonial measures, happened in Andhra region in the form of the Chittoor Palegars' Revolt (1804) the revolt of the Parlakimidi Zamindars (1835-37) and the Narasimha Reddy Revolt (1846).etc. The revolt of the Paiks in Orissa in 1817, the rising of the Gujars under Bijai Singh talukdar in Kumaun and Gahrwal (1824) also were the result of the general dispossession of the traditional feudal elites of the time.[9]

The increasing indebtedness of the peasantry and its exploitation by the money lenders also triggered many such rebellions. The Sanyasi rebellions (1763-1800) in East Bengal, the Kol revolts (1831-32) in Chhotanagpur and the Santhal insurrection (1855-56) were conducted against the agents of the colonial masters. Similarly, the Mopilla revolts in the nineteenth century Malabar were against the implementers of the oppressive colonial policies. The Khasi resistance movement in the Sylhet (1829-1831), the revolts in Malwa (1831); and the Khond insurrection in Ganjam (1846) were all indicative of the anti-colonial tendencies of the landed aristocracy and the peasant classes.

While the settlement of land rights provided the basic context for the numerous violent revolts during the pre-1857 phase, the commercialization of agriculture through the introduction of cash crops and plantations also gave enough reason for the discontentment of the peasants. The numerous Indigo Revolts are a case in point. Many of these uprisings opposed the planter Raj by not only refusing to grow indigo but also refusing to pay taxes.[10] Places like Saran, Tirhut, Munghir, Bhagalpur and Purnia witnessed such revolts by Indigo growers. A significant revolt of the Indigo growers was led by the Wahabi leader, Titu Mir in 24 Parganas of Bengal (1831).

Another instrument of colonial oppression that precipitated the matters towards anti- British revolts was the monopoly merchant capital and a series of unfair measures in matters of trade. The East India Company appointed its own agents for trade and passed regulations that made indigenous trade almost illegal. This resulted in the Khurda revolts against salt laws and the Chakmas disturbances (1782) in the Chittagong region. Thus, besides the land tenures and tax policies of the Company administration, even the policies affecting agriculture, forest laws and trade practices in commodities of daily use also impacted the numerous revolts during the pre-1857 phase. However, the revolts due to the disruption of land relations were more severe, violent and even protracted as land symbolized greater access to authority in the traditional rural scenario.

## Revolts in South India

The anti-British revolts in the south date back to 1757 when in the Madura and Tinnevelli districts, the Eastern Palegars led by Kattabomman Naik and the Western Palegars under Puli Thevar revolted against the British authority. Though the revolt was put down by the British in 1761, the leader of the revolt, Kattabomman became almost a mythical hero and a large fund of literature has grown around him eulogizing his reckless valour and the commitment to the mother country with which he fought against the British.[11] In 1761, a military adventurer, Yusuf Khan led a revolt against the British in the Madurai region.[12] A major revolt occurred in the Coimbatore area in 1800-1801, under the Maruthu brothers, which is termed by many as the "first war of independence". As a part of this revolt, the Palegars of Virupakshi, Palani and Eriyodu in the Dindigul area also rose against the English. Though they failed in their attempts, their heroic struggle overawed the British army officers of the day.[13]

In the Malabar and Travancore regions, very significant revolts were led against British power in 1809 by Veluthambi, the Diwan of the Princely state of Travancore and by Kerala Verma Pazhassi Raja in north Malabar.[14] Similarly, in the Karnataka, there were numerous revolts like in Bidnur (1800), Koppal (1819), Bidar (1820), Coorg (1835), Canara (1837) etc. However, the revolt of Rani Chennama of Kittur in 1824 was the most famous of all such revolts.[15] On the same lines there have been revolts in the Seemandhra (Rayalaseema and Coastal Andhra) as well[16]. The purpose of the present exercise is to discuss such anti- British revolts in Andhra during the Company administration.

## Acquisition of Seemandhra by the British

The British acquired the entire Andhra and Rayalaseema (now familiarly called as Seemandhra) in three phases. The first spell was when the entire Northern Circars were acquired in 1766 and in 1788;[17] the next stage was when the Ceded Districts were obtained on the signing of the Subsidiary Alliance treaty of Lord Wellesley in 1800.[18] The third and final phase was the occupation of the Chittoor and Nellore areas along with the Arcot Nawabi in 1801.[19]

## Northern Circars (1766- 88)

The area that constituted Northern Circars formed part of the Kakatiya kingdom for more than two centuries till it was overrun by the Tughlaks in 1323 AD. Thereafter, two kingdoms namely Vijayanagar and Bahamanis were founded in South India. During their period smaller principalities like the Vizianagaram, Rajahmundry and Kondavidu were formed by the Reddy rulers and during their period which lasted till the beginning of the 16th. Century, Telugu culture and literature flourished. Immediately later, Qutub Shahis of Golconda brought the entire Deccan under their sway.[20]

The fall of Golconda in 1687, brought the entire territory under the Mughal rule. But after the death of Aurangzeb in 1707, the Mughal governor in the Deccan, Mubarez Khan was defeated in the battle of Shakar Kheda in Berar by Mir Qamar-ud-din Nizam – ul-Mulk, Asaf Jah I in 1724.[21] A chronicle of the Asaf Jahi rulers has recorded the event thus:

> 1724, September, 30 (Wednesday) A great battle takes place between Mubarez Khan and Nizam –ul- mulk on the plain of Shaker Khera which is renamed, Fatha Khera, resulting in the death of Mubarez Khan.[22]

The Mughal Emperor gracefully confirmed Nizam-ul-Mulk as the Subedar of the Deccan.[23] He took the title, Asaf Jah and thus became the founder of the Asaf Jahi dynasty.[24] As the Subedar, he had under his control the entire Deccan and the Carnatic.

To check the disorders in the Deccan, Asaf Jah I divided his territory in to five Nawabis. They were: Cuddapah, Kurnool, Sira, Savanur and Arcot. In the Coramandal coast, he created five Circars each under a Fouzdar (also called, Amildar), and they were: Chicacole[25], Rajahmundry, Ellore, Murthuzanagar (present Guntur) and Mustaphanagar (Krishna). Under the Fauzdars were the Zamindars. The Zamindars in the Northern Circars had hereditary rights to their respective territories and enjoyed a certain amount of political, economic and judicial powers. They had their military under their control. The military force of the Zamindars was of three kinds: 1, Common peons who were paid in cash and were expected to be always in attendance, 2. the *Mokkasas* who were paid by the grant of land and 3. *Manovrthy* peons who were military tenets of high order who also were expected to bring in their adherents whenever it was needed.[26] The Zamindars usually seized every opportunity to defy their overlords like the Fauzdars or Amildars whenever there was a change of government. In case the overlord was too weak to control them, then the Zamindars gradually declared themselves as independent.[27]

The Circars broadly corresponded to the present districts of Srikakulam, Vizianagaram, Visakhapatnam, East and West Godavaries, Krishna and Guntur in the present Andhra Pradesh; and also the Gajapathi and Ganjam Districts in Odisha. The administration of Chicacole was first entrusted to Anwaruddin[28]. However, in 1742, Jaffar Ali Khan was appointed as the Fauzdar of Chicacole in succession to Anwar.

## French got the Circars First

The English and the French had several factories in the Circars and struggled for commercial control over the region. After the death of Nizam –ul – Mulk, the English and the French took sides in succession disputes at Hyderabad.[29] Finally, Salabath Jung, Nizam –ul- Mulk's son, supported by the French under Gen. Bussy became the Nizam. He ceded four of the five Northern Circars Chicacole, Rajahmundry, Ellore Murthuzanagar (except Mustaphanagar i.e. Guntur) to the French in 1753.[30]

## The British Occupation

The French administration in the Northern Circars was beset with several revolts by the Zamindars of the region and the British who had their commercial interests in several places like Masulipatam, Visakhapatnam, Ingeram etc. naturally came into conflict. Nizam Ali, (1792-1803) who came to the throne at Hyderabad was an open ally of the British and thus the French power started to decline in the Circars. The defeat of the French armies in 1758 by the combined armies of Col. Francis Forde and the Zamindar of Vizianagaram ultimately led to the establishment of the British supremacy in the Circars.[31]

Robert Clive, who by then having won the battle of Plassey in 1757 defeating Siraj-ud-daulah, the Nawab of Bengal, was in a commanding position. Bengal was prosperous and it could easily supply men, money and materials for the success of the Company in its endeavors. Clive was appointed as the Governor of Bengal and the acquisition of Northern Circars was to a large extent due to the active role he played.[32] Clive obtained from the Mughal Emperor Shah Alam, a grant of the Northern Circars in favour of the British East India Company. On 12, November, 1766, a treaty of alliance was signed with Nizam Ali by which the Company's acquisition of the Circars (except Guntur) from the Mughal emperor was confirmed.[33] The British in their negotiations, were ably helped by Kandregula Jogipanthulu, a prominent *Dubasee*. The company on their part agreed to maintain troops for the

Nizam's assistance. Guntur, which was a personal estate of Basalat Jung, the Nizam's brother was to remain during the life time of Basalat. After Basalat Jung died in 1782, the British finally acquired it in 1788. Thus all the Circars came under the sway of the British.[34]

The French administration in the Circars and the way in which their power was reduced leading to the triumph of British diplomacy in the acquisition of the Circars in 1766 is dilated in the Chapter on the Revolt of the Vizianagaram Zamindars, as they played a leading role in the rise of the British power in the Circars.[35]

## Acquisition of Rayalaseema (1800)

After occupying the Northern Circars, the next important acquisition of the British was the Rayalaseema region with the exception of Nellore and Chittoor which were a part of the Carnatic . The Districts of Cuddapah, Kurnool, Anantapur and Bellary (but later Bellary went to the Karnataka State) which came to be known as the Ceded Districts were transferred to the Company as a result of the Subsidiary alliance treaty in 1800.[36] These areas were a part of the territory of the Nizam, but his hold on them was not strong after the death of Nizam-ul-Mulk in 1848. The Nawabs of Cuddapah and Kurnool were frequently attacked by the Marathas who made themselves masters in the regions like Sandur, Penugonda, Gooty, Gurramkonda etc. The Mysore Nawabs like Hyder Ali and his son, Tipu Sultan also conducted several incursions into these parts and by 1790, the entire Rayalaseema area was incorporated in the Mysore kingdom[37]. However, in the third (1792) and fourth (1799) Mysore Wars, the Nizam supported the British with men, money and materials. For the help rendered by the Nizam, he got several territories in the Rayalaseema region in the treaties signed after the Mysore wars. In 1792, the Kangundi Palem, which was in Baramahal, (present Salem),a part of Punganur Zamindari, Kalahasthi and Karvetinagar were got by the

Nizam as his share from Mysore. In 1799 again, he received as his share the remaining part of the Rayalaseema area.[38] But he was not to rule the region for long.

On October, 12, 1800, seventeen months after the conclusion of the last Mysore war, the Nizam entered into a treaty with the British under Lord Wellesley's system of Subsidiary Alliance and ceded to them all the Districts of Rayalaseema in return for the maintenance of a military force stationed by them to give protection. To these Ceded districts was appointed, on 1 November, 1800, Thomas Munro as the Principal Collector[39]. Munro was to become prominent by experiments he conducted in land revenue administration in the Ceded districts that led to the introduction of the Ryotwari System.[40]

## Acquisition of Chittoor and Nellore, (1801)

The Districts of Nellore and Chittoor were a part of the Carnatic Nawabi and were got by the British after dispossessing the Nawab of Arcot. In 1795, Muhammad Ali, (who was actively engaged in the Carnatic Wars) the Nawab of Carnatic died and was succeeded by his son, Omadat-ul-Omrah. The new Nawab cleared all the dues to the Company by taking loans from the moneylenders at exorbitant rates of interest. He had also assigned lands to his debtors and agents who in turn started harassing the ryots in matters of collecting the rents.

When the Fourth Mysore war was declared against Tipu Sultan in 1799, Lord Wellesley, the Governor-General demanded, for war expenses, three crores of rupees from the Nawab which he could not comply. Adding to it, the British felt that the Nawab was in league with Tipu of Mysore. After the fall of Tipu, it was discovered in the searches at Srirangapatam, that the Nawab of Carnatic was in secret correspondence with Tipu Sultan against the British. Thus the Company government found enough excuses to proceed against Arcot Nawab[41].

In the meantime, Omadat –ul-Omrah fell ill and nominating his son, Ali Hussain as the successor, he died. The Company government wanted Ali Hussain to resign his civil and military authority to the care of the Company. On his refusal, the British turned towards Azim –ul-Omrah, the brother of the deceased Nawab. He accepted the conditions and an understanding was signed on 31 July, 1801, by which he handed over the whole of his authority over the Arcot Nawabi in lieu of a pension amounting to one-fifth of the estimated revenues for his maintenance.[42]

Arcot, after the acquisition by the British was divided into two Districts; the Northern Division of Arcot and the Southern Division. For the North Arcot, Chittoor became the headquarters and for South Arcot, Cuddalore was made the headquarters.[43] Nellore and Chittoor being parts of North Arcot, came under the direct control of the British. With the acquisition of these two districts, the occupation of the entire Seemandhra (Andhra and Rayalaseema along with Chittoor and Nellore) was complete.

No sooner the acquisition was over, there were several revolts and rebellions in all the three areas of their acquired territories. If it was the Zamindars, the Hill tribes and the minor Zamindars in the Northern Circars, it was the Palegars and their Kattubadi Inamdars in the Ceded Districts and in Chittoor who defied the British authority and resisted their rule. The way these rebellious Zamindars and Palegars conducted their revolts and the heroic struggle they waged under the East India Company administration' forms as the frame of reference for this study.

## References

1. Archana Prasad, "The 1857 Rebellion: A Pre-History", *People's Democracy, Vol. XXXI*, no. 9, March, 4, 2007.
2. Bipan Chandra, *Rise and Growth of Economic Nationalism,* People's Publishing House, New Delhi, (1966) rept. 1977, p. 34.
3. For details about the important stages of Colonialism in India, Bipan Chandra, " Colonialism, Stages of Colonialism and Colonial State" in

A.V. Srinivasa Murthy, et.al. (Ed.), *Essays on Indian History and Culture,* Felicitation Volume, in honour of Prof. B. Sheik Ali, 1990, pp. 141-162.

4. Rajani Palme Dutt, *Economic History of India* pp. 84-92.
5. Sarada Raju, *Economic Conditions in Madras Presidency, 1800-1850,* Madras, 1941, p. 50.
6. Bipan Chandra, *Rise And Growth of Economic Nationalism in India,* New Delhi, rept. 1977. p. 29. Also see, Sunit Kumar Gosh, *India and the Raj,* Vol. I, Calcutta, p. 44.
7. There were several occasions when the Weavers in the Northern Circars refused to weave for the Company merchants and went on strike. P. Swarnaltha. *The World of Weaver in North Coromandal C. 1750- 1850,* Hyderabad, 2005. pp. 123-124.
8. Sunil Sen, *Agrarian Relations in India, 1793-1947,* People Publishing House, New Delhi, 1979, P.158. The categorization of Peasantry is done by various scholars in a varied way. However, Lenin's categorization is considered to be more scientific; when he says that peasants are divided into: Land lords, Rich Peasants, Marginal Peasants, Poor peasants and landless laborers. See, V.I. Lenin, *Imperialism, The Highest Stage of Capitalism,* Progress Publishers, Moscow, rept. 1983.
9. Archana Prasad, *op.cit,* p. 3.
10. The grievances of Indigo planters persisted till the beginning of the 20th. Century. The Champaran Satyagraha of Gandhi was to launch him into the main stream of national movement. Judith M. Brown, *Gandhi's Rise to Power,* (CUP,) 1972, P.172. Also see, Bipan Chandra, et.el. *Freedom Struggle,* National Book Trust, New Delhi, (first published 1972, rpt. 1983. p. 127.
11. Robert Orme, *A Study of the Military Transactions of the British Nation in Indoostan from the Year, 1745,* (1861).

    A feature film of the 1960s "Veera Pandya Kattabomman", with Shivaji Ganesan in the lead, has made the hero almost a demi- god and the character lives in the minds of the Tamils even now.
12. K. Rajayyan, *South Indian Rebellion,* Mysore, 1971, pp. 128-131 Also see, J. Welsh, *Military Reminiscences,* Vol. I, p. 134-35.
13. K. Gowri, "Rebellions in the Dindigul Region", in S. Gopalakrishnan (ed), *The South Indian Rebellions, (Before and After 1800)* Chennai, 2007, pp. 43-50.
14. T.P. Sankaran Kutty Nair, *Pre- 1857 Upheavals in Travencore,* in S. Gopalakrishnan, (Ed), *op.cit,* pp.63-93.
15. K.R. Basava Raja, "Anti-British Rebellions in Karnataka of The Nineteenth Century,", in S. Gopalakrishnan, (Ed.), *op.cit.* pp. 94-111.

16. The term 'Seemandhra' gained currency in recent times after the agitation for formation of Telanagana as a separate state gained momentum. The Rayalaseema and Coastal Andhra areas are now familiarly referred to as *Seemandhra.*
17. The entire text of the Treaty with Nawab Asoph Jah, Nizam Ali, the Nizam of Hyderabad dated 12 November, 1766, by which the entire Circars were handed over to the British, is given as Appendix II, in this book.
18. The text of the Subsidiary Alliance Treaty signed with the Nizam on 12 October, 1800 is given at the end of this book, in Appendix-IV.
19. The Text of the Treaty with Azim Ul-Omrah, the Nawab of Arcot, is given as Appendix V.
20. Abdul Mazeed Siddiqui, *History of Golconda,* 1956, p. 7.
21. Yusuf Hussain Khan, *Nizam ul Mulk Asaf Jah, I,* 1936, p. 136.
22. *The Chronology of Modern Hyderabad,* Published by the Central Record office, Hyderabad, 1954. p. 1.
23. Sarojini Regani, *Nizam- British Relations,* Hyderabad, p. 63.
24. The name Asaf Jahi is said to have derived from 'Asoph' supposed to be one of the ministers of King Solomon, the Hebrew monarch. See, Henry George Briggs, *The Nizam: His History and Relations with the British Government,* Vol. I (first published 1861) New Delhi, 1985, p. 36.
25. Chicacole (the earlier name of Srikakulam) is said as the derivative of two Persian words, *Chika* and *Khol*. 'Chika' means a small cloth bag which can be closed by pulling a string around its neck. Khol means 'open'. Under the Muslim rule, this place was used as a toll gate where the traders were demanded by the staff in Persian, 'Chikka Khol' meaning "open the bag and pay the toll". For the details, see, D.G. Carmichael, (ed.) *Manual of the District of Vizagapatam in the Presidency of Madras,* Madras, 1869.
26. A.V. Raman Rao, *The Economic Development of Andhra Pradesh, 1766-1957*, Bombay, 1958, p. 5.
27. Zamindars of Vizianagaram and Bobbili, for example, were prominent in the Chicacole Circar. They led the revolts of the Hindu chiefs in Northern Circars even during the Mughal administration. When the English Company established its settlements in the Circars, they were surrounded by the lands of the rebellious Zamindars who were united for the time being putting aside even their hereditary rivalries. For details, V.R. Jagapathi Verma, *Peddapuram Charitra,* p. 130.

28. Anwaruddin, later was elevated as the Nawab of Arcot. However after he was killed in the battle of Ambur (1749) during the Carnatic wars, his son Muhammad Ali and son-in-law, Chanda Sahib contested for the Nawabi of Arcot with the help of the British and the French respectively. See for details, Edward Thompson and G.T.Garratt, *Rise and Fulfillment of the British Rule in India,* Rept. Allahabad, 1976, p. 73.
29. The death of Nizam-ul-Mulk is recorded as follows; 1848, May, 22, (Sunday) Nizam –ul-Mulk passes away at dusk. The Chronology of events records that on the next day, his son Nasir Jung succeeded to the throne as the Nizam. See for details, *The Chronology of Modern Hyderabad, From 1720 to 1890,* published by Central Record Office, Hyderabad, 1954, p.4. However, after the death of Nizam–ul-Mulk, the first Asaf Jah in 1748, his son, Nasir Jung and grandson, Muzafar Jung contested for the Hyderabad throne. After the death of these two during the Carnatic wars, Salabath Jung became the Nizam. For details, see, G. Srinivasachari, *Advanced History of India,* Bombay, 1970, pp. 586-589.
30. This was the first ever grant of a large extent of land (78,000 square KM) to any European power in India. This was also the beginning of the introduction of the "Subsidiary Alliances" in which land was given in lieu of the European military support. This alliance was perfected later by the British, under Lord Wellesley in 1800.
31. M. Venkatarangaiya, *The Freedom Struggle in Andhra Pradesh, (Andhra),* Hyderabad, 1965, p. 17
32. The battle of Plassey was fought on 23 June, 1757. In Fraser's description, "...as the first rays of the morning sun blazed across the field, Clive ascended the roof of a small hunting hut in which he had lain without sleep during the night." So writes about this decisive battle, R. W. Fraser, *British India,* (first edition, 1896), London, 1916, p. 100.
33. For the entire text of the treaty, see, C.U. Aitchison, *A Collection of Treaties Engagements and Sannads,* Vol. V, pp.14-15 Also see, P.R. Rao, *History of Modern Andhra,* New Delhi, 1978, p.18. Also see, Henry George Briggs, *The Nizam: His History and Relations with British Government,* (first published, 1861) Vol. 1, 1985, pp. 83-84.
34. M.S.R. Anjaneyulu, *Vizagapatam District, 1769- 1834: A History of the Relations Between the Zamindars and East India Company,* Waltair, 1982,. Also see, Edward Thompson and G.T. Garrett, *op.cit*, p. 94.

    Nizam Ali made altogether six treaties with the British East India Company during his reign. These treaties are listed in Henry George Briggs, *The Nizam : His History and Relations with the British Government,* Vol. I, (first published 1861) New Delhi, 1985, pp. 83-84.

35. No one valued the Northern Circars more than the British. The Sultans of Golconda, the Nizams and even the disintegrating Mughal Empire gave great importance to the region for its economic prosperity and potentials of trade. M.S.R. Anjaneyulu, *op.cit.*
36. M.Venkatarangaiya, *Freedom Struggle*, op.cit. p. 20.
37. P.E. Roberts, *India Under Wellesley,* p. 57.
38. Edward Thompson and G.T. Garrett, *op.cit*, pp. 200-207.
39. Rev. G.R. Gleig, *The Life of Major General Sir Thomas Munro, Late Governor of Madras*, Vol. 1, London, 1831.
40. For a detailed study of the work of Thomas Munro and his Ryotwari land tenure, particularly the process of classification of lands and assessment based on the classification, See, Nilmani Mukherjee, *Ryotwari System in Madras, 1792-1827,* Calcutta, 1962, pp. 150-222.
41. A. F. Cox, *A Manual of North Arcot District in The Presidency of Madras,* Madras, 1881, p. 73.
42. *Ibid.*, p. 74.
43. For the North Arcot District, George Stratton was appointed as the first Collector, and he went ahead with the introduction of new land revenue policies. It is generally believed that what Munro was to the Ceded Districts, Stratton was to North Arcot (Chittoor) District. Mohammad Mustapha, "George Stratton and the Revenue experiments in Chittoor District" Un–Published M..Phil dissertation, University of Hyderabad, (1990).

## Chapter - II

# Revolts in Ganjam

After the acquisition of the Northern Circars by the Company in 1766, there have been numerous rebellions by the Rajas and the Zamindars in almost every district. The causes for such general discontent among the native chiefs against the British is not far to seek. In the first place, it was the nature of the Company rule that invited trouble. As the dominant motive of the company was to maximise the revenues without any regard to the prevailing conditions in the region, it was but natural that the native chiefs to become restive. The Company needed great amounts of money not only as their profit, but also to conduct various wars and expeditions at that time in India.

It may be seen that the Company servants at that period of time were ignorant of the local customs and the traditional systems of land revenue. Various experiments the Company administration conducted in matters of land revenue collections were seen by the native gentry as a means to fleece them and the Company was looked upon as a body pitted against the well being of the natives.

There was always a lurking fear among the Zamindars that in case they failed to discharge the payments on time, their estates were to be sequestrated by the Company invoking the obnoxious sun-set laws. Thus the hereditary right of the Zamindars which they enjoyed traditionally was threatened.[1] The Company officials also acted ruthlessly for furthering their commercial objectives. This was clearly discernable in matters of the treatment meted out not only to the feudal chiefs and peasants, but even to the weavers and other artisans in Andhra, whose products they bought for exports. There were occasions when the weavers refused to weave cloth for the English merchants and struck work to protest the atrocities of the Company representatives and the copdars[2].

The unscrupulous methods of loom collections, the tyranny of the copdar system and the unfair exercise of political power to coerce the unwilling artisans to work on unattractive wages compelled the weavers to forsake their trade and adopt different ways of life.[3]

The Company administration also was opposed to the Zamindars and other chiefs maintaining their own armies and it felt that the presence of military with every chief was an affront to their power and authority. It was also the considered opinion of the Company officials, that the chiefs sans their army establishments would be amenable to the agreements and for the due discharge of the tributes. But the Rajas and the Zamindars were in no mood to disband the armies as such military establishments were associated with their traditional authority and it was the means to evoke loyalty of the rural peasantry. There have been thus reasons for the conflicts between the Company and the Zamindars on the assumption of the Northern Circars in Andhra.[4]

The consolidation of the British administration over the territories they acquired in Andhra took a long time and this was evidently because of the resistance put up by the local chiefs like the Zamindars in the Northern Circars and the Palegars in the Rayalaseema area. Palegars again were in the Chittoor and Chandragiri region and these areas formed part of the North –

Arcot District during the Company administration. The revolts of the Zamindars in the Northern Circars were the earliest ones as the Circars came under the British much before the Ceded districts and Arcot regions were acquired by them.

The Zamindars in the Districts of Ganjam, Visakhapatnam, Godavari (both East and West Godavari Districts), besides being revenue farmers, also were hereditary chieftains with well garrisoned fortifications and large military establishments.[5] They were descendants of several royal families. Most of these Zamindars were accustomed to oppose any authority and always tried to assert their independence. They also fought with other neighbouring Zamindars and tried to extend their territories at the expense of others. The Zamindars were the first to refuse to fall in line with the British to pay them the tribute. They resented the Company rule and rose in revolts against the British.

During the period of political uncertainty immediately after Northern Circars were brought under the British, all the Zamindars could considerably strengthen themselves. They were prepared to defy the authority of the new dispensation and were in no mood to surrender willingly to the authority of the British power. They were also determined to use their own military in fighting against the Company forces. Almost every prominent Zamindar in the Northern Circars gave considerable trouble to the Company administration.

Apart from the Zamindars in the plains, there were also several tribals in the hilly areas like the Savaras, Khonds and the Bhills who often raided the plains and carried away anything they could lay their hands on. The Zamindars therefore used to appoint a number of Bissoyis to prevent such insurgencies. These Bissoyis were granted lands in lieu of their services and were allowed even to build forts with army men to keep themselves alert to avert any retaliatory attacks of the tribal groups from the hills. The

Bissoyi lands were held generally in the 'Maliahs' and were limited to the Ganjam District.[6]

For almost fifty years after the Company established its authority, it had to use, year after year, its military against the Rajas and the Zamindars in order to collect the annual revenues. There were also several rebellions from the Zamindars of the Northern Circars when the company administration insisted on the payment of the accumulated dues of the tribute. Most formidable opposition in the Northern Circars was from the Zamindars of Ganjam, Visakhapatnam, Godavari (Present East and West Godavari), Krishna and Guntur Districts.

## Revolts in Parlakimidi Zamindari

In the Chicacole Circar of the Northern Circars, there were many powerful Zamindaries like the Parlakimidi, Gumsur, Vijayanagar, etc in the Ganjam District. They gave constant trouble to the Company by defying the regular payment of tribute. Company administration had to resort to military action to bring the rebellious Zamindars and their supporters to order. Among all the chiefs of Ganjam District, the Zamindars of Parlakimidi, proved to be the most fierce and rebellious. This family of Zamindars claimed their descent from the famous Gajapathis of Orissa. At the time when Northern Circars came under the British in 1766, Narayana Deo was the Raja of Parlakimidi. In the subsequent treaty drawn between the Nizam and the British endorsing the transfer of the Northern Circars to the Company in 1768, Narayana Deo's position in relation to the British was made clear. It is pointed out in the treaty that :

> Narrain doo, one of the Zamindars of the Circars of Chicacole, has lately raised disturbances in the Itchpore country and refused to pay his rents or obedience to the Company; the Nabob Ausuph Jah agrees .......to write letters not only to Narrain doo, but to all the Zamindars in the Circars acquainting

> them, that they are in future to regard the English Company as their sovereign and to pay their rents and obedience to the said Company......without raising any troubles or disturbances.[7]

The Zamindar, Narayan Deo was actively engaged in anti-British activities even before the area formally came under the British. Col. Forde, the British commander who was sent by Robert Clive from Bengal after the battle of Plassey, reported as early as 1759 that the Parlakimidi Zamindar was disrupting the supplies to the British forces stationed in Ganjam. Once the Northern Circars were vested to the care of the Company and when his Zamindari was placed under its care, Narayan Deo refused to obey the Company authority.[8]

In 1768, the Company administration having decided to deal with Narayan Deo, sent Col. Peach, who at that time was in command of a British contingent at Masulipatnam to subdue the recalcitrant Zamindar. Col. Peach set out with his army and defeated Narayan Deo in May 1768. He made the Zamindar to take refuge in the hills of the Zamindari. His son, Gajapathi Deo was then proclaimed as the new Zamindar. But Narayan Deo who did not reconcile to his exile came back as soon as Col. Peach left with his army. He then contacted for help, the Marathas who at that time held Cuttack. He also sought the help of Bhima Deo, the Raja of Vijayanagar, another prominent Zamindari in Ganjam.

The new Raja, Gajapathi Deo soon, proved himself more rebellious than his father. In 1772, when there was pressure from the Company officials, he fled from his estate and like his father sought protection under Bhima Deo of Vijayanagar. In order to wean away from his ally, the British resident tried his best to make Gajapathi return to his estate. As all the efforts failed, the British conferred the Zamindar on his brother, Jagannatha Deo. As the new ruler was also rebellious, the British soon replaced him with Gajapathi again. But these frequent changes brought only anger and resentment among the Parlakimidi Zamindars. Gajapathi Deo continued to be defiant towards the Company administration and refused to discharge the tributes due to the government.

In 1798 the Collector of Ganjam issued a proclamation urging all the people of the Zamindari not to help the Raja in his opposition to the Company. The Raja and his family members were kept under military guard. This led to a major insurrection in Parlakimidi. Gajapathi Deo was joined by his brother, Jagannatha Deo in the insurrection. The Collector of Ganjam, with difficulty could separate the two siblings before the insurrection was put down. In 1802, Gajapathi Deo died and the Company recognized his son, Purushothama Narayan Deo as the successor to the Parlakimidi Zamindari. But, Jagannatha Deo laid claims to the Zamindari. As his claims were turned down, Jagannatha Deo resorted to intimidations and started to pillage the Zamindari with his trusted followers. However, in 1804, Jagannatha Deo was captured and imprisoned by the British[9].

Purushothama Deo however died young in 1805. He was succeeded to the Zamindari by his infant son, Jagannatha Gajapathi Deo. The estate therefore was kept under the Court of Wards and one Padmanabha Deo, a close relative of the Zamindar's family was appointed as the regent to help the infant Raja in administration of the Zamindari. The regent was very unpopular and during the period of his regency, there were several disturbances in the Zamindari. They all culminated in the rebellion of 1813 and as a result, the Company administration removed Padmanabha Deo as the regent. There was yet another disturbance in 1816 spearheaded by the disgruntled Padmanabha Deo. The government proclaimed martial law and the rebellion was suppressed[10].

Much of the fighting spirit and the frequent revolts of the Parlakimidi Zamindars against the Company were due to the support they got from the rebellious Bissoyis and their men, popularly known as the Doras in the Zamindari. Adding to it, there were also family rivalry involving the widowed queen – mother, Seriga Mahadevi and others. The Bissoyis and the Doras also were divided as they supported each of the rival groups. There were large scale disturbances throughout the Zamindari. Law and order reached the lowest ebb. As a result, several villages were burnt down by the rival groups and there was virtual anarchy in the entire Zamindari[11].

It was at this stage that the government of Madras appointed in 1832 George Russell as a special Commissioner on the affairs of Parlakimidi. The Commissioner was entrusted with powers even to declare martial law if need be to suppress the rebellion and bring peace and order in the Zamindari. Russell at once set out with a large army to Ganjam and captured all the important leaders who were reported to be fomenting rebellions. During the year, 1833-34, he occupied the important forts like, Guma, Rajagadda, Jeringi etc. Some of these forts were considered impregnable as they were fortified by the rebel leaders. Several other smaller forts were razed to the ground and the leaders were captured. Russell thus was able to put down the Parlakimidi rebellions with a heavy hand. Many of the captured leaders were imprisoned and some of them were publicly hanged. Few others were imprisoned in the far off Vellore fort. By the middle of 1834, Parlakimidi Zamindari was restored to peace.

Parlakimidi witnessed disturbances in later years. During 1856-57, the Savara tribals in Parlakimidi, under their leader, Radhakrishna Dandasena revolted against the Company administration. They plundered several villages and caused large scale disturbances. The Government sent its troops to the interiors of the hilly regions and the Savara rebels were suppressed. Radhakrishna Dandasena was captured and was publicly hanged along with other Savara leaders. It may be noticed that during the Savara rebellion, the Bissoyi chiefs and the Doras in Parlakimidi, who earlier supported the Zamindars against the Company troops, gave support to the English armies in suppressing the Savaras.[12]

## Revolts in Gumsur

Like Parlakimidi, the Gumsur Rajas also gave considerable trouble to the Company administration. The family of Gumsur Rajas was the most ancient and powerful of the Rajas of Ganjam. The Rajas had many strong forts and their army exceeded eleven thousand strong. The Gumsur rajas have famously defied even the French under General Bussy in 1757 by refusing to pay tribute when the Northern Circars were transferred to their control by the Nizam, Salabath Jung. Even after other Zamindars in the Circars surrendered to Bussy, Gumsur continued to defy him. Bussy then had to lead an army to Gumsur to make the Raja to agree to pay the revenue.

During the period, 1759-1767, taking advantage of the prevailing political confusion, the Raja of Gumsur, Kishen Bhanj occupied nearly twenty three Haveli (Government) villages outside of his Zamindari. In 1768, after the first English Resident arrived in Ganjam, on the formal transfer of the Circars to the British, the Zamindar reluctantly surrendered few but retained at least ten such villages[13]. In 1773 Kishen Bhanj died and was succeeded by his son, Vikram Bhanj. The new Raja fomented a series of disturbances against the British. For nearly five years after accession, he refused to pay any tribute to the Company though he collected the revenues from the peasants. This naturally angered the British and in 1778 the armies were dispatched against Vikram Bhanj. The Zamindar was driven away into exile from his Zamindari. But even from his exile, Vikram Bhanj continued to give trouble to the Company administration and even managed to recover few forts occupied by the Company forces. [14]

As pressure was mounted by the British forces, Vikram Bhanj secretly visited Madras in 1779 and unsuccessfully tried to have an understanding with the authorities for reinstating himself as the Zamindar. But the Madras council decided to make Lakshman Bhanj, the brother of Vikram Bhanj as the new Zamindar on the condition of the payment of Rs. One lakh as tribute annually. On the death of Lakshman Bhanj in 1788, his son, Sikhara Bhanj succeeded to the Zamindari. The tribute earlier agreed upon proved to be heavy and the Zamindar could never pay the amounts regularly. This gave rise to several conflicts between the British and Sikhara Bhanj.[15]

In Ganjam, there were several rich money lenders who stood surety for the payment of tribute by the Zamindars and in turn charged exorbitant rates of interest. These Sowcars, as they were called locally, caused great havoc with the connivance of the Company officials and became scourges both for the Zamindars as well as the peasants. Sikhara Bhanj became a defaulter in matters of payment of annual tribute. He also complained of the fraudulent practices of the Sowcars. But when the company mounted pressure on his payments and did nothing to restrain the activities of the Sowcars, Sikhara Bhanj decided to defy the Company and resorted to rebellion.[16]

Sikhara Bhanj got the support in his revolt from the neighbouring Zamindars. Mani Deo, the Zamindar of Vijayanagar and Jagannatha Deo of Prathapagiri with their respective armies, declared their support to Gumsur. Thus it became a formidable combination and the Company had to carry out several operations to put down the revolt. The campaigns went on for more than two years and several forts were captured by the English armies. In 1801, the company issued a proclamation deposing Sikhara Bhanj and declaring his son Dhananjaya Bhanj as the Raja of Gumsur in succession to his father.

Sikhara Bhanj who did not reconcile to the loss of authority continued to give trouble to the Company administration by taking refuge in the hill regions of the Zamindari. When all attempts to capture him failed, the British resorted to conciliatory measures. There was an understanding by which Dhananjaya agreed to hand over few Muttas, (Groups of villages) in the Zamindari to his father for maintenance and in return, the father recognised the accession of his son to the Zamindari.[17] By 1808, Dhananjaya Bhanj asserted his position so well that the father gave up all the Muttas under his control. It is said that Sikhara Bhanj agreed to go on a long pilgrimage leaving both the Company and the son in peace.

Once the trouble from Sikhara Bhanj was over, Dhananjaya Bhanj started indulging in several cruel activities. He murdered his own mother and the step mothers. He fell into arrears of tribute to the Company. When the affairs at Gumsur were going out of control, the Company decided to act firmly with Dhananjaya Bhanj. In 1835 a strong military contingent was dispatched against Gumsur to resume the Estate. Some of the forts in the Zamindari were occupied, but the situation was not improved. The Raja's men gave such trouble to the Company's army that the Collector, who was in charge of operations, wrote to the government of Madras thus:

> The authority of the government is only acknowledged in the District where the influence of the troops extends— the neighbouring Zamindars, the Hill chiefs, the Sirdars, the inhabitants of the country as far as I can judge, and in many instances I suspect, our own public servants are adverse to the downfall of the Goomsur family and the establishment of the power of Government. We have been and are still obliged to draw every article of supply from a great distance. The enemy in small parties commit outrages upon such villages or individuals as are suspected being friendly to our cause.... The object of all parties here is to have a Rajah and unless government is prepared to establish and maintain its power by force, I at present see little hope of a return to tranquility but by establishing a Rajah,[18]

It is very clear by the above assessment of the Collector of Ganjam how formidable was the resistance offered to the Company forces by the Zamindars of Gumsur.

Unable to resist the constant attacks of the Company troops, Dhananjaya Bhanj fled into the Hill tracts and continued to fight against the British armies. But while in the hills, he passed away in 1835. Though their Raja died, the followers of Dhananjaya continued their fight against the British. With the help of the Khonds, who were experts in the gorilla tactics, the armies of Gumsur continued to give trouble to the Company armies. The government at Madras, then decided to put an end to the disturbances at any cost and sent a large contingent of military to suppress the rebellion in Gumsur.

George Russell, who earlier was sent against Parlakimidi was now entrusted with the task of putting down the Gumsur rebels. Russell with his army proceeded against the Gumsur Zamindari and at once occupied all the strong forts like Kallada, Galeri, Durgaprasada etc. The rebels were driven away even from other strongholds. The Company forces then entered the hill areas of the Eastern Ghats and shattered the traditional bastions of the Khonds, who gave support to the Gumsur rebels. Several Khond leaders were captured and imprisoned. By 1837, the entire opposition was silenced and peace was restored in Gumsur.[19]

After the rebellion was put down, Gumsur Zamindari was abolished and it was taken over by the Company administration. The members of the Gumsur Zamindari family were banished from the District and were sent away to Vellore. Several other leaders and supporters were captured and most of them were either put to death or imprisoned for life.[20]

Apart from Parlakimidi and Gumsur other Zamindaries in Ganjam like the Vijayanagara, Prathapagiri and Durgaprasada also gave considerable trouble to the Company administration with their rebel forces. But the Rajas of the above Zamindaries mostly aligned with other Rajas in their rebellions and did not launch any revolt on their own.[21] In addition to the revolts of the Zamindars in the Circars, there were few *'fithuries'* or outbreaks of tribal people. The tribals of Golugonda in the Visakhapatnam region, revolted against the Company and for three years, from 1845 to 1848 they could give great trouble to the government.[22]

## References

1. Erick Stokes, *The Peasant and the Raj*, CUP, Delhi, 1978, p. 2.
2. P. Swarnalatha, *The World of Weaver in Northern Coromandal C. 1750-C 1850*, Hyderabad, 2005, p. 124.
3. A.V. Raman Rao, *The Economic Development of Andhra Pradesh, (1766-1957)*, p. 16.
4. James Grant, Political Survey of the Northern Circars as appended to Volume III, Appendix 13 of the Fifth *Report of The Select Committee on the Affairs of the East India Company*, pp. 3-4.
5. Firminger, Walter Kelly, *Fifth Report of the Select Committee of the House of Commons,* Madras, 28 July, 1812, Calcutta, Vol. II.
6. Bissoyis were the chiefs in the Maliahs in the Ganjam District. See S. Sundararaja Iyengar, *Land Tenures in the Madras Presidency*, Madras, 1933, p. 140.
7. For the text of the treaty dated, 23 February, 1768, see, Henry George Briggs, *The Nizam: His History and Relations with the British Government,* Vol.1, (first published, 1861), Delhi, 1985, pp. 233-241. Also, C.U. Autchison, *Treaties and Engagements* Op.cit, Vol. V, p. 23.
8. Mamidipudi Venkatarangiya, *Andhra lo Swatantra Samaram,* Tel. Government of Andhra Pradesh Publication, Hyderabad, 1972. p. 8.
9. M. Venkatarangiya, *The Freedom Struggle in Andhra Pradesh, Vol. 1, (1800-1905)*, Hyderabad, 1965, p. 24.
10. S.B. Chowdhuri, *Civil Disturbances During the British Rule in India*, p. 143. Also see, Ganjam District Manual, p. 170.
11. Ganjam District Manual, p 175 Also see, S.B. Chowdhuri, *Op.cit,* p. 143.
12. S. Sundararaja Iyengar, *Land Tenures in Madras Presidency, Op.cit,* Madras, 1932, p. 140.
13. M. Venkatarangiya, *Freedom Struggle in Andhra Pradesh, (Andhra), 1800- 1905,* Vol. I, (Hyderabad,) 1965, p. 26.

14. *Ganjam District Manual*, Madras, p. 157.
15. Mamidipudi Venkatarangiya, *Andhralo Swatantra Samaram,* Tel. Government of Andhra Pradesh Publication, Hyderabad, Hyderabad, 1972, p. 8.
16. Lanka Sundaram, "Revenue Administration in the Northern Districts, 1759- 1786", *Journal of Andhra Historical Society,* Vol. VII, October, 1932, p. 75.
17. N. Ramesam, (ed), *Srikakulam District Gazetteer*, Hyderabad, 1979, p. 29.
18. M. Venkatarangiya, *Freedom Struggle in Andhra Pradesh (Andhra)*, Hyderabad, 1965, Vol. I, p. 28.
19. George Russell's Report on " Disturbances in Parlakimidi, Vizianagaram and Guntur, 1832-1836, Tamil Nadu Archives, Vol. (102) ASD, D, 124.
20. Lanka Sundaram, Revenue Administration of Northern Circars, 1759-1786, Journal of Andhra Historical Society, Rajahmundry, Vol. VII. Part. 2, October, 1932, pp. 71-72.
21. Ganjam District Manual, Madras, p. 14.
22. P.R. Rao, History of Modern Andhra, New Delhi, 1978. pp. 18-19.

## Chapter - III

# Vizianagaram Zamindars and the British

Vizianagaram Zamindari, the biggest and the most powerful of all the Zamindaries in the Northern Circars formed part of the Chicacole Circar. The other prominent Zamindaries in the same Circar were Bobbili and Jeypore. While Bobbili enjoyed the same status as that of Vizianagaram, Jeypore had within its jurisdiction, several minor Zamindaries.[1] Taking advantage of the not so strong fortifications of the minor Zamindaries, Vizianagaram raided at various periods of time and brought those Zamindaries under its submission.[2]

### Foundations of the Family

The Zamindars of Vizianagaram had a hoary past. According to the Kaifeeyats, the family of the Zamindars claimed its ancestry from one, Madhava Verma, a Rajaput chief who led his men to the south in the 17th Century. During the rule of the Qutub Shahis of Golconda, one Sher Muhammad Khan was appointed as the Fauzdar of Chicacole in 1652. Madhava Verma, who by then became one of the trusted lieutenants of the Fauzdar, was appointed as the Zamindar of Vizianagaram. Madhava Verma belonged to 'Poosapati" clan and from then the Poosapati family rose to prominence. The kshatriya princes (Rajus) of this region had always great respect to the Rajas of Vizianagaram because of their supposedly Rajaput descent.[3]

By virtue of their proximity to the Fauzdar at Chicacole, and to the Golconda Sultans, the Rajas of Vizianagaram assumed a prominent position in the entire Circar region. At the time of the transfer of Circars to the English, the Raja of Vizianagaram was in possession of the entire Chicacole Circar having subdued other Zamindars like the Bobbili and Jeypore including the minor Zamindars under its protection.

## Early Relations with The English

Even when the early English trading factories came up in the Circars, the Company administration sought the help of the Rajas of Vizianagaram to carry on their trading activities. The English were quite aware that their settlements at Visakhapatnam and Ingeram would suffer if they were not to maintain friendship with the Zamindars of Vizianagaram, who were known to be very powerful.[4] The Poosapati Rajas also needed the support of the English in the furtherance of their own power. The mutual friendship became necessary as the Vizianagaram rulers were also maintaining their own ships for business and trade. This is evident in a letter that Viziarama Raju of Vizianagaram wrote in 1740 and sent through his Vakil, Adiyappa to the English in Madras with a request to help his Vakil in "selling the paddy there".[5] The English also on their part, always responded favorably to the requests of the Rajas of Vizianagaram by providing all the assistance to the Raja's ships in their ports.

During the period of Anglo- French rivalry in the Deccan that resulted in the three Carnatic Wars (1744-1763) there were disturbances in the Northern Circars. As Chicacole was a rice producing area, paddy was sent to the south in ships for sale by several Zamindars. The English suspecting that those ships were meant for the French, used to burn down such ships and seize the money, goods and merchandise. Even in such situations, the Raja of Vizianagaram continued to send his ships with paddy to Madras, with the assistance of the Company officials. Vizianagaram was considered as one of the few "Commercial Families" engaged in grain trade similar to some of the Zamindars in Bengal who were engaged in banking, money lending and sugar manufacturing.[6] Even after Northern Circars were passed on to the French in 1753, Viziarama Raju continued to be friendly with the British because of his trade in paddy.

## Vizianagaram's Relations with Gen. Bussy

For an assessment of the causes for the rivalry of the Vizianagaram Zamindars with the English that culminated in the battle of Padmanabham in 1794, it is necessary to examine the relations the Zamindari had with Gen. Bussy during the period of the French administration of the Northern Circars (1753- 1758). The intense opposition of Vizianagaram to the Company rule, in fact had its genesis during the French occupation of the Circars.[7]

Even before Bussy got the Northern Circars from the Nizam, Dupleix the French governor at Pondicherry was trying to contact the agents of the Raja of Vizianagaram for support. Therefore it is no wonder that Bussy tried his best to win over the friendship of Viziarama Raju who at that time was supporting the British and their trade at the factories in Visakhapatnam, Ingeram, and in other parts of the Circars. Bussy promised Vizianagaram Zamindar all possible military help if only he turned against the British.[8] In the initial stages, both the English and the French vied with each other in trying to woo the Vizianagaram Zamindar as he was the most powerful of all the Zamindars in the Circars. But once the region went to the French, the reputation of the British among the Zamindars, reached the lowest ebb.[9] The English with a view to secure their trading centers brought an understanding between the Zamindar of Vizianagaram and his rival, Jafar Ali, the chief deputy of the Nizam in the Circars.[10]

Soon, Jaffar Ali enlisted a large army, exhorted all the Zamindars including Viziarama Raju and formed a "formidable Union" with a view to oppose the French and to cause troubles in their management of Northern Circars.[11] But as the Zamindar of Bobbili, Raja Ranga Rao, with whom Viziarama Raju had an ancestral enmity, was on the side of Jaffar Ali against the French, Viziarama Raju decided to withdraw from the "Union". Most other Zamindars also deserted Jaffar Ali. At this stage, Bussy arrived in Circars in July, 1754 to settle the revenues. As the Zamindars were well disposed towards the French, Bussy permitted their Sunnads and their hereditary privileges. The Zamindar of Vizianagaram was persuaded by Bussy to take Rajahmundry Circar for a payment of Rs. 13 lakhs a year. He was made a *Mansabdar* of 2000 men and thus he was kept in good humour, like most of the other Zamindars.

## Battle of Bobbili (1757)

The battle of Bobbili that was fought between Bussy, the French general and Raja Ranga Rao, the Zamindar of Bobbili is a significant one in the annals of the History of Andhra. This was the first occasion in the Northern Circars when a native army came face to face on a battle field with a European army. This battle also gave inspiration to the Zamindars to rise against the British in later years. Though Viziarama Raju went out all the way to support Bussy due to Jaffar Ali factor, he was inclined to remain friendly with the English for furthering his trade interests.

In December 1756 when Bussy arrived in Rajahmundry, Viziarama Raju called on him and requested the French support in putting down Bobbili. Many other Zamindars like Kakarlapudi, Satyavaram, Sringavaramkota, Peddapuram, Madgul, Ponnamouda etc. also met Bussy at Rajahmundry. But Raja Ranga Rao did not go to Bussy to meet for, Viziarama Rao was already in Bussy's camp.[12]

Gen. Bussy who was upset at the attitude of Raja Ranga Rao, set out with his troops against the fort of Bobbili and seized it on 24 January, 1757. Robert Orme gives a graphic picture of the defenses of Bobbili. Raja Ranga Rao and his men fought bravely but lost the battle. Raja Ranga Rao was killed and so were many of his men.[13]

## Death of Viziarama Raju

Three days after the seize of Bobbili fort by the French and the death of Raja Ranga Rao in the hands of the French under Bussy, Viziarama Rao the Zamindar of Vizianagaram himself was murdered on 27, January, 1757. Angered by the annihilation of their Raja, Ranga Rao's men killed the Vizianagaram Zamindar in his tent. Bussy therefore had to settle the succession issues in both the Zamindaries. Bussy installed Ananda Raju, a nephew of Viziarama Raju as the new Zamindar of Vizianagaram and in Bobbili, Venkata Ranga Rao, the son of Raja Ranga Rao was made as a Jagirdar of Kothapalle alone.[14] After the Bobbili war, the French domination in Northern Circars under Bussy increased considerably.

After the departure of Bussy from the Circars having settled the revenues, Ananda Raju of Vizianagaram made efforts to expel the French and sought the help of the English. Accordingly he wrote to the Councils at Calcutta as well as at Madras. Robert Clive who by then had defeated Siraj –ud-doulah, the Nawab of Bengal in the battle of Plassey, was comfortably placed in Bengal with men and resources.[15]

Robert Clive immediately sent one of his able followers, Lt. Col. Francis Forde to deal with the affairs in the Northern Circars. Forde reached Visakhapatnam with his armies in October, 1758.

Ananda Raju set out with his troops to the aid of the English army. The combined armies of Col. Forde and Ananda Raju attacked the French troops. In December in 1758, in a final assault at Chandurthi, the allies defeated the French armies. The Chandurthi battle marked the eclipse of the French influence and the ascendency of the English in the Circars. Though Col. Forde occupied the Northern Circars with the help of Vizianagaram, he restored them back to the Nizam of Hyderabad from whom the British acquired in 1766 with a formal agreement followed by a Mughal Firman two years later[16].

## Accession of Viziarama Raju II (1760-1794)

After the victory over the French at Chandurthi, the differences between the English and the Zamindar of Vizianagaram started to surface. Ananda Raju, who was instrumental in inviting Col. Forde and helped the English forces in liquidating the French power in the Circars, died suddenly of small-pox on 25 February 1760. He was succeeded by his adopted son, Poosapati Ramabhadra Raju, renamed on accession, as Viziarama Raju.[17]

At the time of accession, Viziarama Raju II was a boy of twelve years of age. Around that time, Salabath Jung's place was taken by his brother, Nizam Ali (1762-1803) in Hyderabad as the Nizam.[18] The new Nizam took kindly to Viziarama Raju II and on his first visit to the Circars even confirmed him as the Zamindar. Viziarama Raju during his long reign of thirty five years (1760-94) played a decisive role in the affairs of the Northern Circars.

## Diwan Sitharama Raju

In the initial years of his administration, young Viziarama Raju II, was helped by his half-brother, Sitharama Raju who acted as his Diwan. Sitharama Raju was elder to him in age and was very ambitious in nature. He acted in the name of the Zamindar and subdued all the neighboring Zamindars like Jeypore, Kurupam,

Palaconda etc. He took over even Bobbili and imprisoned its ruler, Chinna Ranga Rao. Similarly, the Hill Chiefs of Parlakimidi also were attacked by Sitharama Raju. Next he went against the Nawab of Rajahmundry and occupied his fort. With all these exploits, the power of Vizianagaram Zamindari reached its zenith.[19]

In 1766, when the English became the masters of the Northern Circars, Vizianagaram Zamindari was settled for an annual payment of Rs. 3 lakhs as Peishcush. But the internal administration of his Diwan Sitharama Raju was highly resented by the peasants due to his despotic rule. The nobles and other prominent chiefs in the Zamindari protested and compelled the Diwan to retire in 1775. But a determined Sitharama Raju went to Madras, to obtain the favour of the Governor, Sir Thomas Rumbold to be reappointed as the Diwan.

## Circuit Committee Report

As the Company felt that they were not getting the expected sums of revenue from the Northern Circars, the Directors of the East India Company appointed in 1777 a committee of Circuit to investigate the exact status of the Circars. But the Governor, Rumbold stopped the work of the Circuit Committee in 1779 and wanted all the Zamindars to meet him in person to settle their respective Peishcush amounts.[20] While all the Zamindars of the Circars obliged the Governor's orders and went to Madras, Viziarama Raju of Vizianagaram excused himself on some frivolous grounds but wrote that he was prepared to settle his Peishcush with the Collector at Visakhapatnam. Being unhappy with the tenor of the reply, Rumbold wanted to teach a lesson to the Vizianagaram Zamindar. He at once forced on the Zamindar, the services of the much hated Sitharama Raju, the Diwan, who earlier was removed.

The Directors of the Company who resented the drastic acts of Rumbold in matters of Vizianagaram Zamindari took severe action against the Governor on whom there were several corruption charges. In 1781, Rumbold was removed from governorship. The House of Commons in London in a resolution passed on 25 April, 1782 expressed their displeasure at the conduct of the Governor in dealing with Vizianagaram Zamindari. It said:

> That the Governor did by menaces and harsh treatment compel Viziarama Raj, the Raja of Vizianagaram to employ Sitharama Raj as the Diwan of the Zamindari and that the harsh treatment and compulsive menaces to which the Raj was subjected were humiliating, unjust and cruel and highly derogatory to the honour of the British nation.[21]

The treatment meted out to Viziarama Raju by the governor of Madras made him a bitter enemy of the British. The Circuit Committee however resumed its work of investigation after the dismissal of Rumbold. After touring all the Circars, the Committee submitted its final Report. Among the numerous suggestions it made, the following were the important clauses having a bearing on the Vizianagaram Zamindari:

1. The military forces amounting to twelve thousand at the disposal of the Vizianagaram Zamindari should be disbanded.
2. The Zamindar be allowed to have 760 army-men and 50 horses, besides an additional force of two thousand men to keep a watch on the passes leading to the hills from the plains.
3. The Raja was to pay Rs. five lakhs per year additionally after disbanding the army.
4. Jeypore which was occupied earlier, should be made a separate Zamindari independent of Vizianagaram.
5. The Zamindars who were imprisoned in the fort of Vizianagaram were to be released forthwith.[22]

Viziarama Raju was prepared to accept most of the above clauses but was unwilling for the payment of additional Peishcush of Rs. Five lakhs as he was already in debts. He also removed Sitharama Raju and appointed a person of his choice, Jagannadha Raju as the Diwan. However, Sitharama Raju continued to give trouble to his brother even while in exile. The English were very unhappy with Viziarama Raju as he failed to discharge the payments regularly.[23] Even the Bengal Council advised the government of Madras to take adequate steps to "bring Viziarama Raju to senses."[24]

## Harsh Terms

When the arrears became heavy, the government decided to take stern action against the Zamindari. The government wrote a harsh letter to Viziarama Raju threatening that his Zamindari would be taken over and held by the Company till all the dues were paid. It was made clear that the Zamindar would be allowed to reside at a place of his choice outside his Zamindari with a comfortable allowance for the maintenance of himself and his family.

Even before he could reply to the humiliating ultimatum, the government dispatched its forces and the Vizianagaram fort was occupied on 2 August, 1793. He was allowed a monthly pension of Rs. 12, 000 for his maintenance. His request for an increase in his monthly allowance to Rs. 30, 000 was turned down. The Zamindar was asked to proceed at once away to Visakhapatnam.[25]

## Battle of Padmanabham (1794)

After the government took over Vizianagaram Zamindari, it was divided into three Collectorates and officers were appointed to each of them. But the officers faced problems as no one was willing to come forward to rent the lands for the fear of the Raja. Moreover, there were many chiefs including the hill Zamindars who were loyal to the Raja. Even the peasants and general public were sympathetic to the dispossessed Viziarama Raju.

Col. Pendargast the Commander of the Company forces in Vizianagaram thought that the very presence of the Raja in the vicinity was causing problems and therefore instructed Viziarama Raju to leave at once to Madras. By keeping the Zamindar away, Prendergast thought, it would be easy to bring order in the Zamindari. But the infuriated Viziarama Raju determined to oppose the British. He collected his armies and moved to Padmanabham, a place mid-way between Vizianagaram and Bhimilipatnam. He was joined by all his kinsmen with their followers. Most of his military that was disbanded at the orders of the English also joined the Raja.

The Company forces now faced a large army of Viziarama Raju and the famous battle of Padmanabham was fought on 10 July, 1794. The fierce battle lasted only for few hours in which Viziarama Raju was killed. His close followers took refuge in the nearby hills along with Viziarama Raju's son, Narayana Gajapathi. About 300 followers of Raju lay dead in the battle.[26]

The heroic fight put up by Viziarama Raju and his death on the battle field surprised Col. Prendergast and other Company officials who expected that the Raja would flee for life. The Zamindar, in view of the immense popularity that he enjoyed, was given a state funeral by the British.[27] Sitharama Raju who did not participate in the battle, died when he was moving in the Mangapuram region and his wife is said to have committed sati by burning herself on his funeral pyre.[28] Thus ended in quick succession, the lives of both the brothers who for more than four decades dominated the turbulent political affairs in the Northern Circars.

## Restoration of the Zamindari

Narayan Gajapathi Raju the son of Viziarama Raju and many

hill chiefs who supported him, offered resistance till May,1795. Several local chiefs collected rents from the ryots on their own, and thus defied the Company administration. The English regiments stationed in the Zamindari also felt that it would be difficult to pursue the rebels in the Hills. The British therefore initiated negotiations to pacify Narayana Gajapathi Raju. The orders sequestrating the Zamindari were withdrawn. Narayana Gajapathi Raju was duly declared as the Zamindar of Vizianagaram. However, his territory was much reduced as several Zamindaries like Jeypore, Bobbili, Palaconda, Kurupam, Salur, Chemudu etc. were handed over to the legal hereditary Chieftains. In 1802, when the Permanent Settlement was introduced, Vizianagaram revenues were estimated at Rs. 12 lakhs and the annual Peishcush on Narayana Gajapathi was fixed at Rs. 6 lakhs.[29]

The battle of Padmanabham and the valiant struggle put up by Viziarama Raju remained as a significant reminder of the valour of the Vizianagaram Zamindars in opposing the might of the British. The battle is commemorated in several Telugu literary works. The poignant story of the fall of Viziarama Raju is popular in the form of Ballads, *Harikathas* and other folk narrations in the coastal Andhra.

## References


1. The minor Zamindaries in Jeypore were: Salur, Andra, Pachipenta, Chemudu, Sangamavalasa, Meranghi, Kurupam, Palaconda, Golugonda etc.
2. D.F. Carmichael,, M *Manual of the District of the District of Visakhapatnam*, Madras, 1869, p. 277.
3. The Vizianagaram Zamindars, in the later period had matrimonial relations with the Royal families in Rajasthan.
4. At the beginning of the 18th. Century, when the Company was confining to the trading activities, the officials with a view to win the favour of the Zamindars and to cultivate friendship with them, used to offer costly gifts consisting of rare artifacts brought from Europe, Persia or China. The English chief at Visakhapatnam factory in a letter dated

November, 17, 1712, writes to the Council at Fort St. George that he was obliged to present Anentaraze (Ananda Raju),of Vizianagaram and other Rajas to the tune of 170 Pagodas. Y. Sudershan Rao, *Andhra Between the Empires,* Hanmakonda, 1991, p. 27.

5. Public Consultations, Country correspondence, *Visakhapatnam District, Records*, letter from Khwaja Abdul Rehman, Dt. 16 August, 1740 Received on 18 Nov. 1840. no. 104.
6. In 1748, Viziarama Raju sent his ships of grain to Madras under the supervision of one, Jayanthi Ramaiah with due recommendation of Sampath Rao, the Diwan of Arcot, requesting the English to assist in the disposal of the grain.

   For details about the commercial activities of the Zamindars, See, Sunil Sen, *Agrarian Relations in India,* 1793-1947, New Delhi, 1979, p. 14.
7. Vizianagaram Zamindars followed a policy of expediency with regard to their relations with Bussy. They used the French to settle their scores with their arch rivals in the region. But as far as the increase in payments of rents were concerned, the Rajas always opposed both the Companies.
8. Robert Orme, *History of the Military Transactions of British Nation in Industan,* Vol.I, Madras, p.334. Also, C.S. Srinivasachary, *AnandaRanga Pillai*, 1940, p. 253.
9. Henry Dodwell, *Dupleix and Clive, The Beginnings of an Empire,* p. 89.
10. In 1753, Jaffar Ali was defeated by Viziarama Raju and even placed his guards at Chicacole. Jaffar Ali shut himself in the fort of Rajahmundry when Raju came pursuing him. Thus there was no love lost between the two before the British successfully brought a rapprochement. Records of Fort. St. George: Country Correspondence, Military Department Letter to Viziarama Raju,. no. 264, Dt. 8 November, 1753.
11. A. Martineau, (Translated by A. Cammiiade, *Bussy in the Deccan( Being Extracts from Bussy and the French)*. p. 178.
12. It is pointed out that the Vizianagaram Zamindar paid Rs. 3 lakhs to the deputy of Bussy, one Hyder Jung' to win over the French General's good will.
13. P. Raghunatha Rao and V. M. Reddy, *Andhra Under the British Rule,* Hyderabad, 1975, p. 13.
14. As Viziarama Rao was issueless, his brother's son Ananda Raju was made as the successor. *Visakhapatnam District Gazetteers*, p. 312.
15. Robert Clive with the help of Mir Jaffar defeated Siraj – ud- doulah in the battle of Plassey on 23 June, 1757 and as per the treaty after the war, he got huge amounts of money. H.H. Dodwell, *The Cambridge History of India,* Vol. V, New Delhi, p. 281.

16. H.H. Dodwell, *Cambridge History of India, op.cit.* p. 292.
17. V.R. Jagapathi Verma, *Peddapuram Charitramu*, Tel. p. 121.
18. The Dairy of the events of the Nizam shows Nizam Ali visiting Bezwada and Rajahmundry in 1760, even before getting coronated two years later. *The Chronology of Modern Hyderabad from 1720 to 1890,* Published by Central Record Office, Hyderabad, 1954, p. 27.
19. M. Venkatarangaiya, Freedom Struggle, op.cit. p.
20. *Cambridge History of India,* Vol. V, p. 281.
21. The extracts from the House of Commons, on the dismissal of Rumbold. It is said that Sitharam Raju himself paid an amount of Rs. 3 lakhs to the Governor to be reinstated as the Diwan.
22. Circuit Committee Report, in *Appendices to the Estate Land Act Committee*, Appendix III, pp.58-64, also see, M.S.R. Anjaneyulu, "Permanent Settlement in the Second Division of Visakhapatnam District, A Case Study," *Ithihas*, Journal of A.P. Archives, Hyderabad, Vol. IV, No.2, 1976, pp. 126-136.
23. Fort William – India House Correspondence, Lt. No. 17, political letters to Court of Directors, 14 December, 1792.
24. Ibid, Vol. XVII, Let. No, 208, p. 248, Political letters 18 May, 1792 on the Instructions from the Court of Directors, Dt. 19 September, 1792.
25. Visakhapatnam District Records, Vol.No.3700, *Board of Revenue Consultations*, Dt. 10 May,1794, p. 129.
26. Fort William – India House Correspondence, (Political, 18 August, 1794, para, 2-6.
27. Mackenzie's Kaifeeyath on the Vizianagaram Zamindars,
28. Fort William – India Office Correspondence, Vol.II, Political letters, lr.no. 40, 12 May, 1795, p. 541.
29. K.S.S. Seshan, "Permanent Settlement: The Madras Way", *Proceedings of the Indian History Congress, 49th.Session,* Karnatak University, Dharwad 1988, pp. 339-342.

## Chapter - IV

# Revolts of The Minor Zamindars

The inspiration provided by Revolt of Vizianagaram Zamindar in 1794 led to similar rebellions against the Company administration in several parts of the Northern Circars. The minor Zamindaries like Kasipuram, Palakonda, Golugonda and Mogulturru, and the hill Zamindars in the Godavari District, like Polavaram, Gutala and Kotipalle also revolted at various periods of time.

### Palakonda Zamindar

Polavaram in the Godavari District witnessed rebellions against the British almost from the time of the assumption of the Circars by the British East India Company. In 1793, the Zamindar of Palakonda, Vijayarama Raj led a rebellion against the British which continued for more than three years. The government deposed Vijayarama Raj and made his son, Sitharama Raj as the Zamindar. But Sitharama Raj died within two years and was succeeded by his brother, Venkatapathi Raj in 1798. But Vijayarama Raj, the deposed Zamindar who for sometime was kept in confinement by the British, when released, broke into a revolt in 1811. The government proclaimed Martial law and ultimately the revolt was put down.

By 1828 Venkatapathi Raj fell into arrears in the payment of annual tribute to the government. When all the attempts to recover the dues failed, the government ordered for the attachment of the lands of the Zamindar. This act of the government resulted in widespread rebellions in the Palakonda Zamindari. As the disturbances were on, the Zamindar, Venkatapathi Raj died and was succeeded by his son, Kurma Raj, an infant. One of the widows of the deceased Zamindar looked after the administration as the regent during the minority of the Zamindar.

During the period of the rule of Kurma Raj, there were several palace intrigues in which the mother and the step-mother of Kurma Raj were actively involved.[1] The Mosakadars and other chiefs were also divided among the different factions. There were also few sections which tried to remove Kurma Raj and make his brother as the Zamindar. These internal bickerings resulted in the numerous disturbances in the entire Zamindari.[2]

In 1833, the rebels in the Zamindari carried out an attack on the Amin's (government's rent collecting officer) office in Palakonda and went to the fort at Atsapavalasa, not far from there. The military officer camping there was attacked by the insurgents. At that time, George Russell was in the District with his army. He immediately proceeded to Palakonda and proclaimed martial law. He then marched with a detachment of the army against the rebels and captured all the leaders, including the Zamindar, Kurma Raj. They were all tried by the Court Martial. Some of them were sentenced to death and many were imprisoned for life. The Zamindar Kurma Raj and all his family members were sent to Vellore to be imprisoned.[3]

George Russell recommended to the government that Palakonda Zamindari be restored to one of the sons of Kurma Raj, the deposed Zamindar. But this was declined by the government and as a result, Palakonda came under the direct management of the government.[4]

## Kasipuram

In 1830 Virabhadra Raju, the Zamindar of Kasipuram led a revolt against the British because of the dispute regarding the pension payable to him by the Company administration. The Zamindar collected an army of adventurers loyal to him and went about attacking the countryside. The revolt assumed serious proportions and continued for more than two years.

In 1832, George Russell arrived at Visakhapatnam as a special Commissioner. He dispatched a contingent of army-men against the rebels. The Company troops committed several excesses. They burnt down villages and created panic in their pursuit of Virabhadra Raju.[5] But due to his thorough knowledge of the hilly terrain in which he took shelter, it was not possible for the Company forces to trace the Zamindar.

Russell proclaimed martial law in the area as the disturbances continued unabated and as the rebel chief was alluding. In 1833 Virabhadra Raju was captured by Russell through one of Raju's men, who fell out from the rebel leader and turned a traitor. Virabhadra Raju then was tried by Court Martial and was sentenced to death.[6] But the government reduced the sentence to life imprisonment. The revolt in Kasipuram came to an end with the capture of Virabhadra Raju. [7]

## Golugonda

When Golugonda Zamindari was confiscated by the Company administration for non-payment of annual tribute in 1845, the Adivasis in the hilly tracts broke out in open rebellion. The Zamindari was held by once famous, Bhupathi family. All the hill Sarcars (Chiefs) united themselves to restore the Zamindari to the

Bhupathi family. The hill chiefs who were loyal to the erstwhile Zamindars set up one Chinna Bhupathi, as their Raja.

The peasants and hill tribes in Golugonda refused to pay their rents to the government, closed the roads leading to the hill areas and started plundering the neighboring villages in the plains. For about three years, they succeeded in defying the troops sent against them. In 1848, the government declared a general amnesty and the tribal leaders agreed to lay down their arms. The government sanctioned an allowance for Chinna Bhupathi and his brothers for their maintenance.

## Mogaltturru

Mogaltturru was another prominent Hill Zamindari in the Rajahmundry Circar. Its Zamindar, Tirupati Raju, rose in revolt against the English during 1787- 1791. The Company administration has rented out Mogaltturru Zamindari to one Bhoopathiah much to the discomfort of the Zamindar.[8] Tirupati Raju raised the banner of revolt and with his trusted men, took refuge in the dense forests of Bhadrachalam. As Bhadrachalam then was in the Nizam's territory, it fell beyond the jurisdiction of the Company administration. Thirupati Raju tried to unite all the rebels against the English, but his attempts failed as the English ably cut the supplies to the rebels in the hills. Thirupati Raju, with no hope of coming successful against the English, sent his feelers indicating that he was prepared to surrender on few favorable terms. In response, the Madras Council informed him that he can return to his place only if he could disband all his armed men.[9]

Thirupati Raju, in the conditions he laid, demanded that he be given an allowance of 2000 Pagodas (about Rs. 6000) per month for his maintenance. The government not only rejected granting such an allowance but it ordered for recovery from Thirupati Raju's properties, the arrears due to the government.

It was during this time that the rebellion in Mogaltturru was carried by one, Jagga Raju, the chief of Koppuram, a dependant Jagir in Mogaltturru. The English immediately sent a large contingent to Mogulturru and warned all the renters and peasants not to extend any help to Jagga Raju and exhorted them to help the British to nab him.[10]

It was the time when Tipu Sultan of Mysore rose against the English and the Company armies under Cornwallis were trying to defeat the Tiger of Mysore in the Third Mysore War (1792). Jaggu Raju taking advantage of the struggle in the Carnatic region, proclaimed himself as the "servant of Tipu Sultan of Mysore" and decided to fight the British. The English wanted to nip the rebellion of Jaggu Raju, in its bud. The English manager at Ellore, John Braithwaite, requested the Council at Masulipatam to send more military reinforcements. Therefore, Lt. R. Barclay was sent at the head of a large contingent to Mogulturru. Barclay commissioned one Bhupaiah, a renter to search the houses in Koppuram estate for Jagga Raju. It was rumored that Jagga Raju was taking shelter in Koppuram. Bhupaiah's men were successful in the combing operations and Jagga Raju was captured, though wounded in his attempt to flee.

The English then resorted to intimidations and the entire Koppuram village was set on fire for having sheltered Jagga Raju and his rebellious followers. The leader, Jagga Raju was taken in chains to Perumada and was kept in prison for about a year before he was released in 1793.

Tirupati Raju who started the revolt in Mogulturru, before Jaggu Raju rebelled, having died in 1791, his adopted son, Venkata Rama Raju was to inherit his property. But the government disapproved of his adoption and seized all his properties.[11] It was declared that Mogulturru was forfeited to the Company in view of the large arrears of payments by the late Raja and that the Zamindari was merged with the Circar.

When the Zamindari was thus taken over by the government, the dispossessed renter, Bhoopaiah, who earlier was helpful to the Company in apprehending Jaggu Raju, felt disappointed. He at once, collected an army of two thousand men and rose in revolt against the English. Few other Zamindars like the chief of Palvancha came to the support of Bhoopaiah. But the Company officials took the help of the Kalaparthi to suppress the revolt of Bhoopaiah. When he thought that he was loosing the fight, Bhooaiah escaped with his men into Bhadrachalam forests and made no further incursions.[12]

## The 'Hill' Zamindars

In the Godavari area, most of the Zamindars were in the hill tracts and therefore it became rather difficult to the Company administration to keep track of such Zamindars when they took to rebellions. It was also next to impossible for the Company troops to penetrate into the inhospitable jungles while the native chiefs and their men were familiar with the interiors of these jungles. The important Hill Chiefs in this region were the Zamindars of Polavaram, Gutala and Kottapalle. They were all members of the same family. There were also several chieftains who extended their support to the Zamindars and enjoyed certain amount of autonomy.

The rebellions of the Hill Chieftains to a large extent were caused by the steps taken by the Company government from time to time to collect the rents regularly and to prevent the accumulation of heavy arrears. There were also internal disturbances as these Hill chiefs quarreled among themselves causing annoyance to the government.

In 1785, Dasu Reddy, the Hill Chief of the fort of Nagavaram attacked and took captive of the neighboring Gutala Zamindar along with his mother. Around the same time, two adventurers, Koneti Thammadu and Veeramallu Kannayya attacked the nearby hill fort of Kottapalle. The Company administration viewed all these insurrections as bad precedents and before such revolts spread to other regions, decided to quell them. A large army of seven Companies was dispatched to put down the disturbances. Soon, the seized forts and Zamindaries were restored to the original owners.[13]

## Gutala

In 1788, the tribute from the Hill Zamindar of Gutala fell into arrears. As the Zamindar could not pay the tribute, the government placed Gutala under the neighboring Zamindari, Polavaram and instructed the Diwan of Polavaram to collect the rents from the Gutala peasants. This arrangement was highly resented by the mother of the Gutala Zamindar who acted as the Regent for the minor. She collected a large army of hill men and brought out a 'Fithuri' in 1790.[14] But she was defeated by the troops sent by the Company. The Gutala Zamindari was handed over to her step-son, Mangapati Devu, the Raja of Polavaram.

## Polavaram

The first wave of rebellion in Polavaram Zamindari occurred as early as 1771 when on the death of the Zamindar, Venkartaramu Devu, there were several claimants to the Zamindari. The council at Madras having enquired of the antecedents confirmed one Nagapathi Devu. But the decision of the Company administration caused disappointment for many a claimant, and the chief of Kottapalle, Venkatarayudu raised the banner of revolt against the government. When a strong English contingent was dispatched, against Kotapalle, Venkatarayudu fled from his Zamindari. The entire Kotapalle estate was sequestrated by the Company administration.[15]

Polavaram became restive again after a gap of twenty years. Mangapathi Devu the Zamindar rose in revolt against the British during 1799-1800. He was ably supported by his brother, Vijaya Gopala Devu. The Polavaram revolt was a prolonged one and unlike other rebellions of the hill Zamindaries, it had greater consequences in the region.

The main cause of the revolt in Polavaram was the removal of Mangapathi Devu for failing to pay the tribute to the government. As the arrears went on accumulating, the government ordered for the sequestration of the Zamindari until the arrears were cleared. The brother of the Zamindar, Vijaya Gopal Devu grew wild and he started the insurrection on behalf of his brother. He went to Rampa region, took refuge with a hill chieftain, Linga Reddy with whose help he collected a large force consisting of Koya tribes- men. Vijaya Gopal Devu and Linga Reddy then with their men started plundering the villages of Polavaram. As the rebels came close in the Zamindari, Mangapathi Devu himself joined the rebels.[16]

The Company forces immediately swung in to action and a strong military contingent was sent to Polavaram which captured its fort. But Mangapathi escaped into the Bhadrachalam area of the Nizam's dominions. Martial law was proclaimed in Polavaram and a reward was announced for the capture of Mangapathi Devu. Yet, by 1800, with the help of Linga Reddy, the Koya chief, Mangapathi renewed his insurrections. But his brother, Vijaya Gopala Devu surrendered to the English on the assurance of unconditional pardon. Soon the insurrection in Polavaram abated.

However, the estate of Polavaram was handed over to a relative of Mangapathi Devu. When the Permanent Settlement was introduced in 1802, a new Sannad was issued to the Zamindar and a fresh Peishcush amount was fixed.

There were similar revolts from the Zamindars in Krishna and Guntur as well. During the year, 1768- 69 the Zamindar of Ongole carried out several attacks with the help of his followers. But the

Company administration which took exception to the activities of the Zamindar, sent a large army and the insurrection was put down with a heavy hand.[17]

There was also trouble from the Nuzivid Zamindari. One Padmanabha Rao, a close relative of the Zamindar claimed some Mirasi rights in few villages in Palnad area. Kumara Verma and his son Visveswara Rao had disputes with the government in matters of pension due to them. But all these disaffected Zamindars did not take the rebellious routes to settle the disputes.[18]

## References

1. M.Venkatarangaiya, *The Freedom Struggle in Andhra Pradesh, (Andhra)* Hyderabad, 1965, p.38
2. D.F. Carmichael, *Manual of the District of Vizagapatam Madras, 1869,* p. 277.
3. Vellore (120 Km. west of Madras) had a strong fort and the numerous cells in the fort served as a Central prison during the Company administration.
4. Sir Thomas Munro, the governor of Madras (1820-1827) during one of his visits to Northern Circars in 1822 had made clear that "No Zamindari once forfeited for rebellion should ever be restored". See for details, M. Venkatarangaiya, *Freedom struggle, op.cit* p. 37.
5. Visakhapatnam district Gazetteer, Vol. I, p. 46.
6. Russell's Report on the Disturbances in Parlakimidi, Vizianagaram and Guntur, 1832- 36, ASO, 102.
7. Devireddy Subramanyam Reddy, *Uprising of 1957, Tura Buz Khan, The Hero of Hyderabad,* New Delhi, 2012, p. 35.
8. Mamidipudi Venkatarangaiya, *Andhra lo Swatantra Samaram,* Tel. op.cit, p. 23.
9. Records of the Godavari Collectorate, Correspondence regarding Polavaram Zamindari, 5 July, 1790, Quoted in Y. Sudershan Rao, *Andhra Between the Empires,* Hanmakonda, 1991, p. 146.
10. *Ibid.*
11. *Ibid.,* p. 147.
12. M. Venkatarangaiya, *Freedom Struggle, op.cit,* vol.I, Hyderabad, 1965, p. 39.

13. Devireddy Subramanyam Reddy, *Uprising of 1857*, New Delhi, 2012, p. 36.
14. M. Venkatarangaiya, The Freedom Struggle in Andhra Pradesh, Hyderabad, 1965, p. 38.
15. Y. Sudershan Rao, *Andhra Between the Empires* op.cit. p. 145.
16. M. Venkatarangaiya, *Op.cit*, p. 39.
17. M.V. Rajagopal, Guntur District Gazetteer, Hyderabad, 1977, p. 62.
18. M.V. Rajagopal, Krishna District Gazetteer, Hyderabad, 1977, p. 53.

## Chapter - V

# Thomas Munro and the Palegars

In 1800, when the entire Ceded Districts, with an estimated revenue of sixty three lakhs of rupees a year, was handed over to the East India Company administration, one of the stipulations was that the British government should guarantee the Nizam from any attack. The government of Madras, in their order dated, 24 October 1800, appointed Major Thomas Munro as the first Principal Collector for the " whole of these extensive territories" (Ceded Districts) with four Sub-Collectors under his immediate authority.[1]

For establishing the British authority in the newly acquired Districts, Colonel Arthur Wellesley (the future Duke of Wellington) was asked to move with his armies from Hubli along with another detachment from Mysore in order to meet the " military demands of the principal Collector."[2] But on the assumption of charge, Munro felt that all the Palegars in the area were very turbulent and were not favorably disposed towards the British power. He wrote:

> By every report which has reached me, it appears that almost every Palegar, however insignificant, who had been expelled since the beginning of Hyder's usurpation has been within these few years permitted to resume the management of his District (Palem)."[3]

Thus at the opening of the 19th. Century, there were clear indications for the government to deal with the Palegars who exercised their traditional authority. Munro collected information about all such Palegars. He estimated their number to be eighty in all the Districts, but mostly in Cuddapah. Munro observed that these Palegars, however small, kept up a court, had nominal officers, maintained a small standing army, called as Kattubadidars, who held land grants.[4] Thomas Munro was given every power to bring peace and order in the area. He was also permitted to have direct correspondence with the Governor till the government's authority was well established in the Ceded Districts and that there was no need for his correspondence to go through the usual Board of Revenue.[5]

From the very time of his arrival, Munro recognized the need for crushing the power of the Palegars for ever. He wrote once thus:

> "Before we can draw our revenue undisturbed from willing subjects, we have to remove many powerful and turbulent Palegars and many petty ones of modern origin, who have taken advantage of the troubles of the times in order to withhold their rents for a few years, and then to declare themselves independent. The reduction of these vagabonds, who are a kind of privileged highway men, will render us much more able to resist our external enemies."[6]

Munro carried out his operations so quickly and effectively that by March 1801, the revenues of the Gurramkonda division in Cuddapah district were settled. He also made a proclamation declaring that "every chieftain who garrisoned a fort, maintained an armed force or levied contributions would be treated as a rebel."[7]

Immediately on the Collector's proclamation, in May, 1801, Major–General Campbell, marched against Vemula in the

Pulivendula Taluk and reduced the Palegar to submission. His fort was razed to the ground. On the orders of Munro, Campbell proceeded from there to Pullampeta and forcibly reduced the Metla Chief of Chitvel.[8] These acts of suppression of the Palegars, though the governments at Madras and also at Calcutta approved, the Court of Directors in London, found fault with Munro's policy towards the Palegars. The Directors wanted the Palegars to be upheld in their right and enjoyment of the soil and felt that gradual course of a good government would wean them from "their feudal habits and principles". But for this Munro in his reply ably defended his course of action saying that their feudal habits and principles "consisted of only crimes and oppressions; and if allowed to be continued, would render good government impossible."[9] The Court of Directors was silenced with the reply of Thomas Munro and he went ahead in suppressing all the rebellious Palegars and their armed constabulary.

Munro had in the beginning, only a limited number of troops at his disposal. So he used to deal with the rebel Palegars with caution. In one of his dispatches, Munro writes: I was not prepared at the time to enforce my demand, and I, therefore took no notice of his (rebel Palegar's) conduct". But when he had enough troops at command, such a rebel Palegar was chased from place to place and his fort was destroyed[10]. The first eighteen months of Munro's administration in the Ceded Districts was completely taken up against the Palegars.

## Action Against Uppalur

The usual method adopted by the Palegars and the general reaction from Munro were almost the same in case of the majority of the Palegars' rebellions. "First the Palegar refuses to pay the rent; he becomes a refractory or absconds, and he ends up by being captured, his estate is confiscated, and he is confined in the fort of Gooty."[11]

The way the rebellious Palegar of Uppalur, in the Gurramkonda division of the Cuddapah District was dispossessed by Munro is an example of how the Palegars were dealt with.[12] The Palegar of Uppalur, located about eighty miles west of Cuddapah refused to obey the summons sent by Munro to personally meet him to get the rents settled, when Munro himself was on a visit to Gurramkonda. The Palegar also did not relinquish the two government villages that he has unauthorisedly occupied. Munro took no notice of him till a contingent of troops under Major-General Campbell arrived in the vicinity. Immediately he sent his Thahasildar to take possession of the two government villages, he held, for which there was no resistance whatsoever.

Munro permitted the Palegar to keep his hereditary village of Uppalur on the condition that he would in future be more obedient to the Company administration. But on his arrival, Munro found that the Palegar neither came in person to meet him nor sent the Karanam of his village with the accounts, while other Palegars of Gurramkonda were all present.[13]

Munro decided to act against the Uppalur Palegar, who had a small army of his own with Kattubadidars. He then asked Col. Legar, Commandant of the army at Kamalapuram, near Cuddapah, to send a detachment against the rebel Palegar. The Colonel personally marched with his troops and in a surprise night attack, took the Palegar a prisoner, without any loss of lives. Munro put him in confinement in the fort at Gooty and allowed him a life pension.[14]

## Revolt of Vemula Palegar

In proceeding against the different chiefs who were in arms and withheld their revenue, Munro took measures against those who had no proper title to their possessions. Among such was the Palegar of Vemula, who defied Munro's directions and ultimately was put down. Munro himself narrates about it in his dispatch to the Board of Revenue. According to him, the predecessor of the Palegar of the Vemula was expelled in 1766 by Hyder Ali of Mysore. When that Palegar died, one of his distant relatives seized the Palem. On his death in 1799, the head peon and other servants have put up an old blind man as the Palegar and kept him under their check. When this pretender Palegar was repeatedly summoned by Munro, and when he openly defied the Collector, Munro instructed General Campbell to take action against the Vemula Palegar. The General then sent a force which attacked the fort of Vemula and made the Palegar a prisoner. As Munro himself has stated, "the gates of the Fort were blown open. All the Palegar's men in arms were also imprisoned. However, the Palegar was allowed a pension."[15]

## Other Palegars

After the attack on Thornekal in the Adoni division of the then Cuddapah District (later Adoni was transferred to Kurnool District) there was in 1803, a rebellion of one, Sultan Khan who collected an army of few hundred horse and suddenly appeared on the northern borders of Cuddapah District. His idea was to capture Cuddapah by a *Coup de Main.* Thomas Munro had the prior information on the movements of Sultan Khan, and sent a body of forces which confronted Sultan Khan's cavalry. In the fight that ensued, several of the followers of the rebel leader were killed and Sultan Khan himself was taken a prisoner.[16]

In 1804, there was an attempt to seize the fort of Bellary and also a conspiracy among the Palegars of Adoni to occupy the fort of Gooty with the intention of handing it over to the Marathas, with whom the British were at war. This plot was discovered in time and all the chiefs behind the plot were arrested. While the enquiry was going on, another Palegar with a contingent of nearly 500 seized the fort of Kotakonda in the Cuddapah district and pillaged the village. After looting the village, he captured the village headman, the Patail and also a Kavalgars (Guard) and severed their heads with great contempt. He also killed four or five other villagers and wounded about six very severely before escaping. Though the Collector immediately sent a contingent of troops to apprehend the rebel Palegar and his army, it was not possible as they ably escaped.[17] These incidents of rebellions indicate the turbulent character of the chiefs and their military contingents. These rebellions were mostly against the revenue policies followed by the Company administration and the government's attitude in dealing with the Palegars who lost their traditional rural stronghold. It has taken a long time for the British with their armed forces to bring them to order. [18]

By the time Munro laid down his office as the Principal Collector towards the end of 1807, the Palegars in the Ceded Districts to a large extent were brought under control. The government of Madras while appreciating the services rendered by him as the first Collector of the Ceded Districts, observed thus:

> "From disunited hordes of lawless plunderers and freebooters, they (Palegars) are now stated to be as far advanced in civilization, submission to the laws, and obedience to the Magistrates, as any of the subjects under the government. The revenues are collected with facility; everyone seems satisfied with his situation."[19]

This was very much akin to the changed feelings of the Court of Directors, who earlier had a critical view of the methods Munro adopted against the Palegars. In a dispatch the court of Directors profusely acknowledged his "ability and skill as a Collector"[20].

## Murder Of Macdonald (1832)

Though the Palegars, to a large extent were reduced during the period of Munro itself, there were many instances of rebellions in the Ceded Districts and one such was the murder of Macdonald, Sub-Collector in Cuddapah in 1832. But unlike the revolt of the

Palegars who never wanted to submit themselves to the new revenue regulations of the government and who resisted the loss of the power they were used to enjoy, the murder of Macdonald was the result of a riot that erupted in the town, Cuddapah in 1832. It was the act of a frenzied mob in the backdrop of a supposed sacrilege at a place of worship. Though it was given a religious colour, the revolt evidently assumed an anti- British significance as a high British official was targeted and murdered in broad day light by a mob.

Macdonald, was the Additional Sub-Collector of Cuddapah, and he became a victim of a riot that occurred on 15 June, 1832. Early in the morning, it was discovered that a small pig was killed and thrown bleeding into Cuddapah's main mosque, Jumma Masjid.[21] The Muslims, particularly the Patans, "the most daring and easily excitable of the citizens of Cuddapah", immediately became restive and violent. Soon, an excited mob gathered at the market place and in the bazaar streets. Their numbers soon swelled into thousands. By 10 o'clock in the morning the crowds became so large and frenzied, that the Additional Sub- Collector, Macdonald sent a message to Lacon, the Collector, who at that time was staying in Madanapalle.

Madanapalle, (at present in Chittoor District) was then the summer resort of the Collectors of the Cuddapah District. European officers even from the days of Thomas Munro used to live there during the summer months to escape the torrid climate of Cuddapah. Weddenburn, was the Collector who built the sprawling " Collector's Bungalow" in Madanapalle, where Lacon was staying at that time.[22] In his express message, Macdonald informed the Collector that the crowd was very violent and that he would try to pacify them so as to bring peace in the town. He also indicated that if there was any necessity, he would send for the military from the local cantonment.

After sending the message to the Collector, Macdonald reached his office in a Palanquin. All his subordinates in the cutcheri have assembled and were in great panic. Macdonald who was now convinced that the situation was really grave, decided to press the military to act. He asked for a contingent to arrive at once from the cantonment. Before such a contingent could arrive, Macdonald received a letter through a messenger, from a well known missionary, Mr. Howell who lived in the middle of the town. Howell had expressed a great apprehension of his own safety as he feared an attack on his house by the frenzied mob. Macdonald, in spite of the protestations of his own staff at the office, decided to do his best to help the hapless Missionary. He went to the bazaar accompanied by few of his servants. A naik and few treasury guards followed him. The military contingent he requested for, was yet to arrive.

The moment Macdonald reached the main bazaar, his presence served still more to excite the crowd that has assembled there. The entire crowd pounced on the Sub-Collector, and he was killed. The treasury guard who accompanied Macdonald, when tried to defend, was also killed. The few revenue peons who were with the party of Macdonald, ran away from the scene. The last blow on Macdonald is said to have been inflicted by a Patan butcher. After this unexpected turn of events. the entire mob disappeared within minutes leaving on the spot the dead bodies of Macdonald and his faithful servant . The military contingent, which Macdonald had requisitioned earlier, arrived only to take away the dead bodies of the victims. The Collector, Lacon, also arrived from Madanapalle by that evening. He got some of the rioters arrested and after a trial, five of the ring leaders were publicly hanged[23].

J.D.B. Gribble, the compiler of the Manual of Cuddapah District in 1875 gives a critical assessment of the role of Lacon, the Collector, on his return from Madanapalle. Himself, an Acting

Sub-Collector, at the time of compiling the Manual, Gribble's contempt for Lacon was such that he calls him "the tardy Collector". Gribble felt that Lacon only tried to exaggerate the entire episode. He writes:

> "The Collector (Lacon) endeavored to magnify thus into a preconcerted rising of the Mohammadans with intent to massacre all the European residents, but it is clear that it was nothing more than a sudden outburst of fanaticism to which Macdonald generously, but injudiciously, exposed himself"[24].

However, C.F. Brakenbury, a latter Collector of Cuddapah, in the revised edition of the District Manual that he compiled in 1915, while recounting all the major events of the murder of Macdonald as narrated by Gribble, has added a poignant fact that this young Additional Sub-Collector was twenty four years of age and that his newly married wife survived only few days after his untimely death. Unable to overcome the grief, she died on the twenty first day after the violent murder of her husband..[25] The murder of Macdonald was the most serious crime that occurred in the Ceded Districts subsequent to the suppression of the Palegars by Thomas Munro. But after a lapse of about fifteen years, there was a major revolt brought out by Uyyalawada Narasimha Reddy, a Palegar, in 1846 which attracted the attention of the entire British administrative machinery, as the revolt was on an unprecedented scale. The details of this revolt are discussed in a separate chapter.

## References

1. The government of Madras, in the appointment letter (24 October, 1800) also explained the particulars of the treaty of Subsidiary alliance by which the territories were Ceded to the British. See for the text of the Treaty, Henry George Briggs, *The Nizam, His History, and Relations with the British Government*, (First published, 1861) New Delhi,1985, Appendix- A, No. XXVIII pp.279 – 287; Also, *The Freedom Struggle in Hyderabad (A Connected Account)., Vol. I, (1800-1857),* Hyderabad, 1956, Chapter I, pp. 1-9.

2. Arthur Wellesley was the younger brother of the Governor General, Richard Wellesley. Both of them played a key role in the defeat and death of Tipu Sultan in the fourth Mysore war just a year ago (May 1799). Col. Wellesley later as the Duke of Wellington, defeated Napoleon in the famous battle of Waterloo in 1815. Duke of Wellington's house in London, "Aspley House", is now converted into a museum. For details, see, Edward Thomson and Garret.
3. Letter from Thomas Munro to the Board of Revenue, Quoted in C.F. Brakenbury, Opcit, 46.
4. The Kattubadi Inamdars were not paid in cash, but they cultivated the Inam lands. For details see, K.S.S. Seshan, *British Role in Rural Economy,* New Delhi, 1989, pp. 143-144.
5. J.D.B. gribble, *A Manual of the District of Cuddapah*, Madras, 1875, p. 107.
6. Immediately after being appointed as the Principal Collector, Thomas Munro wrote to the government on the need to take stern steps to put down the Palegars, who he said were mostly on the Cuddapah District. See for details, G.R. Gleig, *Life of Major General Sir Thomas Munro, Late Governor of Madras*, London, Vol. 1, 1831.
7. C.F. Brakenbury, *Opcit*, p. 48.
8. Chitvel has been the seat of the Metla Chiefs who are credited to have built the Rajagopuram at Govindarajaswamy Temple in Tirupati.
9. Thomas Munro's reply to the letter of the Directors, dated, 22 February, 1805, Quoted in C.F. Brakenbury, *Op cit*, pp. 48-49.
10. The method used by Munro was to remove the Palegar, settle the rents with the individual ryots and grant them the *pattas.* So there was no general resentment of the public towards the collector. See for details about the methods used by Munro, G.R. Gleig, Thomas Munro, London, 1831, p.
11. Munro generally allowed the Palegars to be on the run for some time before making any attack. This allowed him time to assemble the troops from different parts of the Districts. G.R. Gleig, *Op cit*,
12. Robert Sewell (Author of Forgotten Empire) Collector of Bellary has printed a valuable Memorandum of Munro's dated March 1802 giving the history of eighty Palegars in the Ceded Districts and stating how he had dealt with each of them. Quoted in ,John Bradshaw, *Sir Thomas Munro,* Oxford, 1906. p. 113.
13. C.F. Brakenbury, *Op.cit,* p. 50.
14. *Ibid.*

15. For details of the Munro's account on Vemula Palegar, see, T.H. Beaglehole, *Thomas Munro And the Development of Administrative Policy in Madras, 1792- 1818*, CUP. 1966, p. 63.
16. *Bellary District Gazetteer*, pp.45-50, also, see. M.Venkatarangaiya, *The Freedom Struggle in Andhra Pradesh, op.cit.* p. 41.
17. J.C. Dua, "Nature of Poligar Revolts in the Ceded Districts during the First half of the Nineteenth Century : A Case Study," in *Indian History Congress Proceedings of the Thirty Fifth Session,* Jadavpur, (Calcutta), 1974.
18. J.D.B. Gribble, *A Manual of Cuddapah in The Presidency of Madras,* (Madras,) 1875, p. 110.
19. C.F. Brakenbury, op.cit. p. 50-51.
20. Extracts from the Letter dated 6 November, 1805 from the Court of Directors, Quoted in C.F. Brakenbury, *op.cit*, p. 51.
21. It turned out later, according to one version, that the dead pig was actually a bandicoot, and was purposefully placed by a Musalman, only to foment trouble. In the Enquiry Commission that was constituted to probe into the Wahabi conspiracy in Hyderabad under Mubarez- ud - Doulah, the brother of the Nizam, the Commission has pointed out in its report that one of the Moulvis in the service of Mubarez has willfully threw a dead pig in the Mosque in Cuddapah, to create hatred against the British. See for details, Enquiry Commission Report, "Mubarez – ud- Doulah and the Wahabi Movement". In Freedom Struggle in Hyderabad, Vol. I, Hyderabad, 1956, pp. 124 -154.
22. Madanapalle, popularly known as "Poor Man's Ooty" "Pensioners' Paradise", etc. came under the newly formed Chittoor District on 1 April, 1911. It is about 120 K.M. from Cuddapah and is known for its cool and salubrious climate. Thomas Munro, the first Principal Collector of the Ceded Districts (1800-1807) was the first European officer to set up residence here to stay during the summer months. He built a thatched Bungalow, for his use in the mission compound in the town. See, K.S.S. Seshan, "A brief History of Madanapalle", *Ithihas*, Andhra Pradesh State archives Publication, (Hyderabad, 1979,) p. 17.
23. C.F. Brakenbury, Opcit, p. 172.
24. J.D.B. Gribble, *A Manual of the District of Cuddapah in The Presidency of Madras,* (Madras) 1875, p. 112.
25. The unfortunate death of the wife of MacDonald is narrated only in the Manual compiled by Brakenbury. For details, see, C.F. Brakenbury, *op.cit,* p. 172.

# VI

# Thornekal Revolt: 1801

The Revolt of Thornekal village in the Adoni division of present Kurnool District in 1801 was one of the first major revolts against the Company administration by the native rural peasantry during the early phase of the British rule in the Ceded districts.[1]

The Rayalaseema region was known as the land of Palegars. The Palegars had about 100 to 200 villages each under their direct control. With their *Kattubadi Inamdars* and other military, they controlled law and order in their jurisdiction[2]. From the period of Vijayanagar empire, they were authorized to collect land revenue from the villages and remit to the sovereign, retaining a portion for the trouble they took for such collection. These Palegars maintained their own armies and extended military help to the kings whenever needed. But after the decline of the Vijayanagara Empire by the middle of the 16th. Century, the Palegars became almost independent.

The conditions under which the Inams were acquired under the successive sovereigns by the Palegars in the Ceded Districts are well described by William Thackeray, in 1807 when he writes:

> In the anarchy and plundering that prevailed from 1788 to 1799, the Potail or the Kurnum acted like a little prince in his

> own village......In most parts of the Ceded Districts, the Potail or the head Rayet, and the Karnum so peaceable in other provinces had become captains of bandits garrisoning independent Castles. In these conditions, one man's gain was another man's loss, and although Inams functioned to preserve village elite, that elite was doubtless subject to much internal revolution.[3]

With the defeat and death of Tipu Sultan in 1799, the area came under the control of the Nizam of Hyderabad. But later with his signing of the subsidiary alliance treaty on 12 October 1800, the entire area was ceded to the British East India Company. Thus the Districts of Cuddapah, Kurnool, Bellary and Anantapur called as the *Ceded Districts,* comprising of the Rayalaseema area came under the Company administration.

In November 1800, Thomas Munro was appointed as the Principal Collector of the newly acquired Ceded Districts. To help him in administrative matters, four Sub-Collectors were appointed and they were placed at places like: Harpanahalle, Adoni, Cuddapah and Cumbam. It was William Thackeray who as the sub-Collector at Adoni, had to confront the Thornekal revolt as the village was within his jurisdiction.

## Impact of New Land Policies

Immediately on taking charge of the Ceded districts, Thomas Munro decided to bring all the Palegars under control and disbanded their military establishments. The responsibility of collection of revenue was directly taken over by the Collector. He then made experiments with the new Ryotwari land tenure and successfully implemented in the area. Though Munro felt that his system of land revenue was more indigenous than the Cornwallis system of Permanent settlement, it was also beset with numerous disadvantages to the farmers. The main drawback was the stipulation that the land rents were to be paid in cash. Heavy taxation became order of the day. The Pattas which Munro is credited to have formulated and got issued for the first time, were meant more to pin down the farmers to the lands they were ascribed. When the peasants became defaulters, their lands were auctioned off. With such strict regulations of the government, the peasants were the worst affected. The revolt of the peasants of Thornekal, in the Adoni division stand testimony to their intense opposition for the new land revenue policies pursued by the British.

## The genesis of the Revolt

Muthukur Gowdappa was the formidable leader of the Thornekal revolt. He belonged to the shepherd community and under his leadership the peasants who were subjected to heavy land taxes, rose in rebellion. In early 1801, the peasants of the region refused to pay the rents that were arbitrarily imposed by the company administration and took to their conventional arms and revolted.[4]

Thornekal got its name, according to the Kaifeeyats, because of a pious Yadava lady, *Thairuni*. This area was traditionally a Yadava dominated area. Yadavas were basically a cattle-rearing community, claiming their descent from Lord Krishna. They wielded political significance and their chiefs ably defended from the successive invasions of outsiders. They also had the reputation of defending their own liberty. During the period of the Vijayanagar rulers, they were at the pinnacle of their powers as the Palegars of the region.[5]

Under the rule of the Palegars, Thornekal area was a part of Kotakonda, one of the *Panchapalems* i.e. five Palems. The other four being, Pathikonda, Devarakonda, Kappatrala, and Maddikera.[6] It is said that this area was politically dominated by the Yadavas even before the establishment of the Vijayanagar empire. Nandyala, Yadavani (present Adoni) were powerful centers for the

Yadava rulers. The villages like Pekkanda, Venkatapuram, Vallapuram, Musurupalle, Daddonapadu, Thornekal etc. were all thus formed by the Yadava chiefs.

## Historical past of Thornekal

Thornekal as a Yadava stronghold, has a hoary past. The people of this village were known for their valour and for their fighting spirit. They have participated in a number of battles in the past to resist external aggressions and resisted any external oppressions. When Aurangazeb, the Mughal emperor invaded Kurnool and Nandyal regions in 1668 and appointed one Bhimsingh as the chief of this entire area with Adoni as his Jagir. It is said that when Bhimsingh tried to subdue the neighboring areas, the villagers of Thornekal, resisted such Mughal attacks and after laying seize to Thornekal for nearly 40 days, the armies of Bhimsingh were to withdraw. The people of Thornekal thus had the reputation for preserving their spirit of unity and freedom with zeal. The entire village depended on agriculture and cattle rearing. The village was well fortified as there was a high protective fort-wall running around the entire village with an imposing gate-way and also a poston gate in the rear part of the village.[7]

As Thornekal and the neighboring village, Pasaladinne, were traditional rivals, they always feared each other. The village youth in Thornekal were always told by the elders to be prepared and vigilant for any aggression from outside. Muthukur Gowdappa, the village chief himself was well trained in all the martial arts in vogue like the 'stick swinging', sword fighting, dueling, horse riding etc. Being a widower, he gave considerable time in spending with the youth at the village centre every evening, in giving training in such martial arts. He used to exhort the young men to protect the village, its people and properties even at the cost of their lives. He used to narrate the stories of great heroes of the lore who laid their lives for the cause of public good and for the protection of the fellow peasants in the village.

## Background of the Revolt

At the time when the Ceded districts were transferred to the Company administration in 1800 and when Thomas Munro became the first Principal Collector of these districts, the Village Thornekal was headed by Muthukur Gowdappa. (Gowda means head or Chief).[8] Gowdappa was highly respected in the village of Thornekal and he was famously known in the local lore, as a descendant of a revenue collector who fought against the oppressive rule of the erstwhile Nawabs and was executed. The Thornekal village was settled by the Company administration and was to pay a stipulated amount of Rs. three thousand annually. The government also appointed one Anki Reddy as the *Munsif* and Shankarayya as the *Karnam* (Accountant) for the purpose of collecting the revenue from the peasants. Both of them had great respect for Gowdappa, the head of the Village. Gowdappa was almost the father figure for the village,

The entire Kurnool district generally falls under an arid region. In the western taluks like Pattikonda, Alur, Adoni and Kodumur, the rain fall was much less compared to the Eastern taluks like, Nandyal and Atmakur.[9] For about 6 years before this area came under the control of the company, all the western taluks of Kurnool were reeling under severe famine conditions due to lack of rains. The peasants could not pay the land taxes as the crops completely failed. The poor peasants ate Prickly pear and such other obnoxious forest produce to keep their bodies and souls together. There were also several starvation deaths reported.[10]

The new British administration was keen to collect land taxes with no concessions whatsoever. The revenue inspectors were instructed by the company officials to be strict in matters of collection of land dues without any mercy. One, Srinivasa Rao the *Ameen*, for the region to which Thornekal was appended frequented the village and demanded the Munsif and the Karnam to pay the enhanced revenue to escape the wrath of the

Company's administrators.[11] But Muthukur Gowdappa, the head of the village, told in no uncertain terms that it has been the custom under the earlier successive Palegars to have exemption from the payment of land taxes whenever the crops failed due drought. But Srinivasa Rao, much to the consternation of Gowdappa, constantly pressurized the village officials. Whenever he came to Thornekal, he came in the company of few peasants from the neighboring village, Pasaladinne, with whom Thornekal was known to have traditional rivalry.

## Reasons for Rivalry

Thornekal and Pasaladinne, though were the neighboring villages, there was rivalry between them. This fact becomes central to the revolt of Thornekal as the murder of the three people from Pasaladinne by Gowdappa and his men finally led to the entire conflict. At the annual festivities of venugopalswamy temple, located in the vicinity of these villages, the Thornekal youth always won the competitions against the Pasaladinne youth, in rural games, sports and martial arts. This was also a reason for the peasants of these villages to be not in friendly relations with each other. Pasaladinne villagers found an opportunity in the impending rift to settle their old scores with the people of Thornekal.[12]

## Company finds a Cause

With a view to pressurize the village officers to pay the stipulated revenues, Srinivasa Rao the Company agent went to Thornekal with few Pasaladinne village leaders. These were the people who revealed the exact amounts of revenue that the Thornekal paid to the earlier governments under the Mysore Sultans and under the Nizam. For Gowdappa and other leaders of the village, the presence of the people from Pasaladinne in their village itself, became objectionable. There were intense arguments and altercation between the two groups. In the melee, Gowdappa was exported into a rage for the unnecessary interference of the Pasaladinne people in the affairs of their village when they were demanding for a right cause, and assaulted the leaders of Pasaladinne. When there was an attempt to retaliate, they were overpowered by others and the three leaders of Pasaladinne, were beaten to death. The names of the three murdered were: Byluppala Rami Reddy, Ganjihalli Sunki Reddy and Pasaladinne Narappa. Their bodies were buried near Thornekal at the orders of Gowdappa, without being handed over to their family members. Srinivasa Rao, who escaped from the scene, went straight to Adoni and reported the matter to the Company officials.[13]

## Thackeray Arrives With Army

William Thackeray, the Sub- collector when he came to know of the murders, was exported to a rage and decided to teach a lesson to the 'recalcitrant people' of Thornekal and its chief, Muthukur Gowdappa.[14] He felt that it was an affront to the very Company administration not only in disobeying to pay the dues, but to attack and murder the people of Pasaladinne who went to the aid of the Company agent, Srinivasa Rao. He at once called upon his army and proceeded against Thornekal.

## Thornekal Prepares For Self Defense

When the news of the march of the army under William Thackeray towards Thornekal reached Gowdappa, he lost no time to assemble all the villagers and apprised them of the imminent attack by the British Company's forces. He exhorted them that they have to rise to the occasion and defend the honour of their village at any cost . The village youth swore that they would fight against the British army and will never yield to any intimidation. They took out all their weapons like the bows and arrows, axes, knives, catapults etc[15]. The high protective fort wall was kept in good repair. Large quantities of gravel were stored in heaps on the ramparts of the fort-wall to be used in catapults. All women and children of the village were sent out to their relatives' houses in the nearby villages. Gowdappa ensured that sufficient food grains to last for months were securely stored .There was also sufficient water in the village well. All the villagers kept a vigil by lighting the bonfires in the village.

## Seize on Thornekal

William Thackeray summoned a fresh contingent of one thousand army- men from Bellary, where the British troops were stationed under the command of Major General Donald Campbell. At the command of the army, Thackeray moved from Adoni to Thornekal. He kept the army at Kadivella, a nearby village and proceeded to Thornekal.[16] He summoned the Munsif and other village officers and apprised them of the need to pay the land rent at once or else, he said, that they have to face the consequences. But as the village chief, Gowdappa made it clear that there was no way to yield to the pressures of the Company officials, Thackeray hurried to Kadivella village, and returned with his army.[17]

The peasants of Thornekal under the leadership of Gowdappa were prepared for any eventuality. They closed the heavy entrance gate of the village and started attacking the army of Thackeray with swords, with bows and arrows, with the deadly catapults, and by pouring-over hot oil from above the fort walls. Thackeray and his army tried their best to breach the fort-walls to enter the village but the efforts proved to be not so easy.

## Break through for the British army

It was at this stage that some leaders of Pasaladinne, who were angry at the murder of three of their men by Gowdappa, came to help the Company forces. They provided a vital information that the postern gate at the northern side of the village was not that strong.. Thackeray immediately dispatched a small contingent which, with little effort smashed down the northern gate. The troops forced themselves into the village and swooped on the people.[18] They started shooting down every one who came on their way. The chief Gowdappa, with a sword in hand was seen attacking the surging army men with all his might. His acts of valor gave an inspiration to the youth who valiantly fought with the invading forces. But with superior arms, the Company forces outwitted the natives and soon, Gowdappa along with Rami Reddy, the Munsif and Shanakarappa the Karnam, were captured by Thackeray's men. Many of the villagers were killed in cold blood.. All the houses in Thornekal were burnt down and reduced to ashes.[19]

The captured leaders, Muthukur Gowdappa, Rami Reddy and Shanakarappa were tied to a tree in the centre of the village. Thackeray decided that Gowdappa and other two leaders should be put to death as a warning to others. He sent round his thalaries to announce in the neighboring villages through *Tom Tom*, that all the three leaders of the rebellion would be hanged on the next day. In the presence of a large gathering, they were hanged to death at the entrance gates of the village.[20] More poignant scenes were witnessed when at the orders of Thackeray, all the dead bodies of those who lost their lives in the revolt, were dumped in an open- well, known as *Kukkalabavi,* without any formal funerals. Several women, who earlier were sent away before the revolt broke out, when returned committed suicide by jumping into another well, *Giddaiah* bavi.[21]

## Munro on Thornekal Revolt

Thomas Munro, the Collector of Ceded Districts, while writing to the Board of Revenue about the 'Thornekal affair' in which 'Mr. Thackeray nearly lost his life', says that the initial murders in the village were done on 20 November, 1801 and that he heard about it on 27th. November (1801). He states that he immediately announced one thousand rupees as reward for any one who could nab the Patel, (Muthukur Gowdappa) on whose orders the murders were committed. He further writes that : "The murders (of three men from Pasaladinne) seem to have originated in private revenge." To substantiate this view, he says: "It was necessary to raise the rent of the village to a fair level to that of others in similar circumstances. The people who brought forward the information required for this purpose are those who have been murdered."[22] About the actual events leading to the incident, Munro had this to convey to the Board of Revenue.

> The Village, Thornekal, like most others in the country, is fortified. The Patel refused to agree to the increase proposed.... instead of obeying, he (Patel) shut the gates, manned the walls, and murdered in the Cutcheri, the three men who had given statements of the produce. These unfortunate people, when they saw the pike men approaching to dispatch them, clung to safety about Sheristhadar, which was the cause of his receiving some accidental wounds. Thackeray who was encamped near the village, hastened to the gate, and on being refused admittance attempted to get over the wall. The men above threatened, and called out to him to desist, saying that they have taken revenge of their enemies, but had no intention of opposing the Sirkar; and he at length, very properly withdrew to his tent. This is the account given (to) me by a peon who attended him"[23]

Thornekal was rebuilt by 1804 and the then Amildar, Bhima Rao was instrumental in the rebuilding of the village. Hence in gratitude of the benefactor, the village, for some time was called as *Bhimapuram* . But later, it was reverted to its original name, ' Thornekal'[24].

The revolt of Thornekal peasants under the leadership of Gowdappa against the enhancement of land revenue by the

Company administration within a year of their assuming power in this region, served as a great inspiration to the people of entire Rayalaseema. The heroic struggle they carried and the supreme sacrifices they made by laying down their lives became legends and the rural folk in this region, even at this distance of time, remember with great admiration the valiant struggle the villagers of Thornekal have put up.

Even today in Thornekal, the village youth, sing 'kolatam' songs in which a group of men dance and sing to the beat of sticks in a rhythmic manner, eulogizing the acts of their ancestors . One such kolatam song translated, reads thus:

> Dazzles bright with shining Rays— Thornekal
> The Abode of great Heroes – Thornekal
> Here lived Warriors of repute – Thornekal
> They ate half a bread —Drank mere salt water
> Yet gave a strong fight—Thornekal
> Gulped burnt-rice — survived on plain water
> Yet kept the entire folk together
> Upheld the aura of divine Madhava Swami
> The Deity that presides our place— Thornekal [25]

## References

1. Dharani Ramachandra Rao, *Kurnool Mandal Charithramu,* Tel. (Pattikonda, 1936), rapt. Kurnool, 2001, p. 58-59.
2. *The Bellary District Gazetteer,* Madras, 1904, p. 176.
3. Erick Stokes, *The Peasant and The Raj, Studies in agrarian Society and peasant rebellion in colonial India,* CUP. New Delhi, 1978, p. 50. William Thackeray was the first Sub- Collector of Adoni, in whose jurisdiction, the Thornekal Rebellion took place in 1801.
4. Y. Raghu, "Thornekal Rythanga Poratam, 1801", *Proceedings of the Thirtieth Session of Andhra .Pradesh. History Congress,* Siddipet, 2006, p. 199.

5. Dharani Ramachandra Rao, *Kurnool Mandala Charithramu,* (Tel), 1936, rept, Kurnool, 2001, p. 56.
6. At present, Thornekal form part of Devarakonda Mandal in Kurnool District.
7. S.D.V. Aziz, *Tharinekanti Muttadi,* Tel. Kurnool, 2008, p. 15.
8. The term, Gowda has Kannada origins. But in parts of Kurnool and Anantapur districts, the Gowdas are in prominent numbers. And even now they are a power to recon with.
9. M.V. Rajagopal, (ed), *Kurnool District Gazetteer,* Hyderabad, 1974.
10. Y. Raghu, *op.cit,* p.200
11. One of the reasons given for the discontent of the peasants of Thornekal was that the Karanam and the Patel of the village were summoned through the Amina Srinivasa Rao, to Adoni, in order to settle the revenues on the Village, for which they were not willing. See for details, Dharani Ramachandra Rao, *op.cit*. p. 57. However, Thomas Munro, the Principal Collector, in one of his dispatches to the Board of Revenue, refers to Srinivasa Rao as the *Sheristhadar.* See, John Bradshaw, *Sir Thomas Munro,* Oxford, 1906, p. 116.
12. S.D.V. Aziz, *Tharinekanti Muttadi,* op.cit. p. 69.
13. In the Report sent by Munro to the Board of Revenue, it is pointed that the Sheristhadar (Srinivasa Rao) was "accidentally" wounded in the scuffle, though the three "unfortunate" men were murdered. Quoted in John Bradshaw, *Sir Thomas Munro*, Oxford, 1906, p. 116.
14. Y. Raghu, "Tharinkallu Rythanga Poratam", *A.P. History Congress proceedings*, *Op.cit*. p. 200.
15. S.D.V. Aziz, *Tharinekanti Muttadi, Kurnool*, 2008, p. 68.
16. K. Maddaiah, *Freedom Movement in Rayalaseema*, New Delhi, 2012, p. 44.
17. Dharani Ramachandra Rao, *Kurnool Mandala Charithramu*, op.cit, p. 58.
18. S.D.V. Aziz, *Therinikanti Muttadi*, op.cit, pp. 62-64.
19. Dharani Ramachandra Rao, *Kurnool Mandala Charithramu*, Kurnool 2001, op.cit. p. 59.
20. Aziz gives a graphic description of the poignant scenes witnessed at the site of the hanging of the three leaders of the revolt before a large gathering. Aziz also writes that the seize lasted for nearly two weeks. But this is not corroborated in the writings of Munro to the Board of Revenue. See, S.D.V. Aziz, op.cit. pp. 71-72.

21. K. Maddaiah, *Freedom Movement in Rayalaseema,* New Delhi, 2012, p. 45.
22. When Munro writes that " The people who brought the information about the produce of the lands" indicate that there were informants for the Company in such matters. Munro also interestingly narrates in the same dispatch to the Board that, "On November, 22 two days after the affair at Thornekal, three Potails and Currunums were murdered by another Patel of Adoni (division) for giving true statements to the Sirkar Servants." See, John Bradshaw, *Sir Thomas Munro*, Oxford, 1906, p. 116.
23. *Ibid.* pp. 116-117.
24. Dharani Ramachandra Rao, op.cit, p. 59.
25. Y. Raghu, "Thornekal Rythanga Poratam", *op.cit*, p. 201.

## Chapter - VII

# Chittoor Palegars' Revolt: 1804

The Palegars of South India, unlike the Zamindars, had different stature and origin in different parts, devoid of any uniformity. They were mostly present in the erstwhile territory of the Vijayanagar empire. But their influence and the power they wielded depended on the nature of their relations with their immediate overlords after the fall of the Vijayanagar. While the Ceded Districts came under the control of the Company in 1800 with the signing of the Subsidiary alliance by the Nizam, Chittoor as a part of Arcot was acquired by the Company administration, as discussed earlier, after dispossessing Azim –ul – Omrah, the Nawab of Arcot, on 31 July, 1801.[1]

The Carnatic Nawabi, after the acquisition by the Company administration, was divided into two Districts: the Northern Division of Arcot and the Southern Division of Arcot, the river Pennar, serving as the dividing line. For North Arcot, Chittoor was made as the head quarters; while Cuddalore was the headquarters for the South Arcot District. George Stratton (1801-03) was appointed as the first Collector of the North Arcot.[2]

North Arcot had within its jurisdiction altogether 13 Taluks. There were few Jagirs, like Arani, Avalkonda, Desur and

Chengalpattu. There were Zamindaries like Kalahasthi, Karvetinagar Venkatagiri, Sydapur and Kangundi. The Chittoor and Chandragiri taluks had Palems, besides Mamandur, Krishnapuram and Karkambadi, which were also Thana (Kaval) Pollams. [3] In the areas which were under the control of the government, the Collector George Stratton tried to introduce a system that was similar to the one that Thomas Munro was trying in the neighboring Ceded Districts. The distinguishing feature of it was that revenues were collected by the government directly through its own servants.[4]

The Chittoor Palems as they were familiarly referred to, were altogether ten in number. They were as follows: 1.Bangari, 2.Thumba, 3 Naragallu 4. Mogarala, 5. Pullur, 6. Gudipati, 7 . Pakala, 8. Yedaragunta, 9. Pulicherla, and 10. Kalluru.[5]

These Palegars were mere Kavalgars or local Constabulary force, during the Vijayanagar period and were in charge of maintaining law and order in the their jurisdiction.. They enjoyed *Inam* lands in return of their services and their positions were hereditary. They also had the right to collect rents. These chiefs, taking advantage of the unsettled political conditions during the period, assumed the title, "Palegar" and began ruling their 'Palems' as though they were almost independent.

The period between 1740 and 1770 saw an unprecedented growth of the influence of the Palegars in the entire south India. These chieftains made vast additions to their privileges through several methods. They often encroached on the jurisdiction of the sovereign or had the consent of the villages and some times had the approval of the Nawabs.[6] As this area witnessed frequent changes in the suzerain masters like the Golconda Nawabs, the Maratha chiefs, the Mysore Nawabs, the Nizam of Hyderabad and the Arcot Nawab, before the English finally took control, the Palegars assumed every power and became masters of the people under their rule.

The Chittoor Palegars revolted against the British within three years after the area was transferred from Arcot Nawabi to the Company administration. Their revolt in 1804 became an inspiration and a trend setter for many a local chief who opposed the British land policies. One of the reasons ascribed to the outbreak of the more severe Vellore Mutiny in 1806 was the presence of the Chittoor Palegars in the prison cells of Vellore fort after the failure of their revolt in 1804.

## The Reasons For The Revolt

There were several reasons for the Chittoor Palegars to feel frustrated about the Company administration that led to their revolt in 1804. In the first place, they resented the manner in which the Arcot Nawab, for whom they had their allegiance and loyalty, was dispossessed in 1801. Adding to it, Stratton after being appointed as the Collector, introduced a new system of land revenue by which he started renting out by villages on an annual lease. When Stratton was succeeded in 1803, by David Cochrane, who earlier had some experience with the Ryotwari system in Balaghat, he wanted to get the survey done for the purpose of getting a fixed Thirwa (Money assessment).[7]

The Palegars in the District looked with apprehension the steps taken by the successive Collectors in introducing the Villagewar and the Ryotwari systems. They were also reluctant to remit the land rents to the new masters. The first two Collectors, George Stratton and David Cockburn, consistently removed several of the rights the Palegars traditionally enjoyed. The Kavali (police) powers of the Palegars were abolished. The Amaram and Kattubadi Inams were all confiscated by the government. The Inams granted to the Kattubadidars when sequestrated, the constabulary forces were highly displeased as they were denied of their livelihood. The lands of other followers of the Palegars and the village officers were also confiscated much to their consternation. The Palegars were asked immediately to disband their armies.[8] Their 'forts' and other military establishments were destroyed. They were even categorized as 'dacoits' and accused as 'highly lawless'[9]. In the confiscated lands, David Cockburn introduced in 1803 the survey and made revenue settlement directly with the peasants on the lines of Munro Settlement in the Ceded Districts, which later was termed as Ryotwari Settlement.[10]

When George Stratton took charge as the Collector of the district, the Palegars initially showed some restrain and were in moderate behavior. But they became restive when the Collector went ahead to raise their tribute and confiscate their privileges.[11] The clause VI of the government's proclamation in 1803 stated:

> The amount of land rent to be paid by the ryots of the Pollums of Chittoor, shall be in future defined by fixed pattas, in order that they may be freed from vexatious demands, to which the ryots have been hitherto subject..[12]

Apart from the above, there was also a strong desire of the Palegars to preserve their independence, for which they were accustomed under the earlier dispensations. The curtailment of their importance and the loss of authority over the Inamdars consequent on the cancellation of the Inam lands, had angered all the Palegars. With the exception of the Gudipati Palegar, all other Palegars declined to pay the enhanced rents, fell into arrears and started to plunder the neighboring Palems.[13]

## Open Defiance of the Palegars

Though the revolt began in June 1803, the rebellious attitude of some of the Palegars was discernable even by the early preceding year. The Palegar of Thumba, in April, 1802, instigated an attack on one Captain Nuttal, who was traveling through his Palem. Most of the other Palegars also were indulging in such acts of violence.

In June, 1803, the followers of Naraganti Palegar attacked and plundered Uttanthangal, a neighboring village. The Collector, Stratton on enquiry, was told that the attack was at the behest of the Palegar himself and that he had his own share in the booty. The Collector also got information that the same Palegar and his party even had a clear plan, before attacking Uttanthangal, to raid Chittoor, the headquarters of the district and loot the treasury there[14]. But they desisted from "such an attempt due to a bad omen," the Collector was told.[15]

Cockburn, the successor of Stratton also had several reports about the violent activities of the Palegars and therefore suggested to the government that "prompt and decisive measures should be taken" against the rebellious Palegars. He even suggested that a military march could be conducted to demonstrate the strength of the British forces. But as the troops at that time could not be spared and as the Commander of the garrison in the Fort at Chittoor, considered his troops were too small for such a show of strength, the proposal was dropped.

Stratton, to prove that he was serious about putting the Palegars to order and punish the recalcitrant ones who did not clear the rents due to the government, arrested the Naraganti Palegar, as he did not clear his dues. But Cockburn, the successor Collector, after taking a promise that he would clear all the dues within twenty days, released the Palegar. But when the promise was not met even after the expiry of the stipulated period, the Collector dispatched a letter of remonstrance. When the bearer of the letter approached the Palegar's fort in Naragallu, 'the Palegar's men in arms surrounded from every side and insultingly made him to carry back the letter to the Collector, who sent it.'[16]

The government of Madras, was stunned at the act of 'perfidy and show of resistance' by the Palegar and instructed at once to resume the entire lands and *rusums* of the Naraganti Palegar. As a follow up, on the orders of the government, on 6 July 1804, a battalion of troops was dispatched to Chittoor to enforce its order. The resolution of the government was announced in a circular addressed to all the rest of the Palegars in the hope that it would serve as a warning to them.[17]

The Company troops under the command of Lt. Col. Darley, arrived at Chittoor from Madras on 17 July, 1804. A company of pioneers also accompanied the army to destroy the forts, fastnesses and other battlements of the Palegars. It was also to open up the remote parts in the Palems by constructing roads. Cockburn then sent an announcement to the Palegars informing that a military contingent has arrived in Chittoor to deal with the rebellious Palegars. However, in the same announcement, he also made it clear that if the Palegars attended on him personally and made arrangements to pay all the dues, their protection and safety were assured.

None of the Palegars attended the office of the Collector, but they sent their Vakils to represent. The reasons the Palegars gave to the Collector for their 'absence' was indicative of the scant respect they had for the authority of the British administration. For example, the Palegars of Bangari and Yedaragunta " were on a fast", the Pulicherla and Kalluru Palegars informed that they have taken for "physic".[18] Others also had some frivolous excuse for their absence thus exhibiting their utter disregard for the Collector. The Vakils were asked to execute an undertaking on behalf of their Chiefs, but the Vakils refused to sign any document with the Collector as they were not authorized by their respective Palegars.

## Collector's Ultimatum

Stunned by the audacity of the Palegars and the stand taken by their Vakils, the Collector issued certain conditions to the Palegars through their Vakils. According to the conditions imposed by the Collector, the Palegars had to pay within eight days half of the arrears along with interest; and the remaining amount within thirty days. If they failed, they have to surrender the land equivalent to the balance. The government would pay a subsistence allowance to the Palegar during the period of resumption of the lands and the Palem would be restored on the clearing of all the payments. If these conditions are rejected by any Palegar, the Collector made it clear that their Palems would be sequestrated and the Palegars punished.[19]

## Occupation of Mogarala And Pakala

In reply to the severe conditions imposed by the Collector, the Palegars of Mogarala and Pakala initially asked for two months time as the condition of eight days was too short; but later both refused to comply and decided to defy the Collector's order.[20] The Palegars immediately started collecting their followers and arming them with a view to resist the Company's authority.

On 25 July 1804, the British battalion under Col. Darley which was stationed at Naragallu, marched to Pennamari, near Mogarala and made preparations to attack Mogarala fort on the next day. But by the evening, the Palegar, declared that he was prepared to cede two thirds of the lands towards the arrears of the payment. When Col. Darley was optimistic of the solution, the Palegar of Mogarala escaped in the night with about 800 to 1000 of his followers. As a result, the British occupied both Mogarala and Pakala Palems. (both these Palems were under the same Palegar as the Pakala Palegar was a minor). The forts and other military establishments at both the Palems were destroyed. A proclamation was issued on 26, July announcing all the Palegars about the occupation of Mogarala and Pakala, and assuring the people, ryots, the peons and others that they had no cause for any concern. Two days later, the Palegar of Mogarala surrendered along with the boy Palegar of Pakala. After their surrender, Cockburn wrote to the government that the Palems would be held by the government and a suitable maintenance allowance will be paid till a permanent settlement was introduced.

> ...until the resources of the country (Palem) were ascertained and a permanent revenue was fixed upon these resources, the Pollums shall remain in the hands of the government and an allowance be made for the maintenance of the Palegars. Should their conduct show them to be deserving of it, they might be delivered on the condition of a Zamindari tenure subject to the regulations.[21]

Thus in order to keep the Palegars away at a distance during the period of "temporary assumption" of their Palems, the Palegar of Mogarala was sent in custody to Vellore and the boy Palegar to Chittoor. Later, both of them were sent to the fort of Chengalpattu.

## Attack on Kalluru and Pulicherla

Cockburn then turned his attention to other rebellious Palems. On 31 July, 1804, he instructed Col. Darley to take steps for assumption of the Palems of Kalluru, Pulicherla, Bangari, Yedaragunta, Pullur and Thumba as these Palegars have not acceded to the terms of settlement proposed to them. On 4 August, a final warning was sent to the Palegars except those who have already accepted the terms, that as soon as the British armies approached the Palems, each of the Palegar was to give the acceptance to the terms already laid out by the government. The terms listed were as follows:

1. To relinquish 2/3 of the lands in the Palem to the British till all the arrears with interest was paid.
2. To consent to a survey of his Palem with a view of farming a permanent revenue.
3. To relinquish all the police powers to the care of the British.

4. To assist the government in destroying all forts and barriers in his Palem.
5. To stop collecting road duties and duties on trade
6. To abolish collection of road customs in the Palem and
7. To agree to pay implicit obedience to the officers in the Sirkar (Government)[22]

As the Palegars did not agree for any of the above terms, Col. Darley and his army proceeded northward against Kalluru and Pulicherla in Chandragiri taluka. On hearing of the approach of the British armies, the Palegars with their followers fled into the nearby jungles. Their forts and *'durgs'* were destroyed; and their estates were taken over. The government then issued a proclamation asking the Palegars to surrender promising personal safety if they submit on their own.

## Pullur, Strongest of All Palems

After destroying the forts of Kalluru and Pulicherla, the British forces turned their attention towards Pullur Palem. On August 7, 1804, the British sent an emissary, Balaji Row to know about the designs of the Palegars. He got the information that the Palegars of Bangari, Pullur, Kalluru, and Yedaragunta were busy in preparing with their arms and ammunition, and were concentrating all their collective forces at a hill near Kaligaripalle. Balaji Row met the Palegar of Pullur who initially consented to relinquish his lands equivalent to the balance that he owed to the government. But later, he said that he was unable to pay due to the failure of monsoon. He also contented that the debts he incurred were due to the rise of Peishcush by the earlier Collector, Stratton. The Palegar thus refused to pay the arrears or hand over any lands in lieu of payment. He also asked the emissary Balaji Row and others to 'leave his Palem.'[23]

Col. Darley then decided to march against Pullur. The Palegar by then had assembled his army of 500 to 800 to defend the fort.

It is said that the Palegar had obtained a solemn promise from the army that they would stand by him till the end - the promise they faithfully kept up. They opened fire on the British army as soon as they were spotted near the fort. It is said that the Pullur armies ably defended the first barrier of the fort with utmost obstinacy till almost the evening. When the Company forces made an assault, the Palegar escaped with his trusted men to the nearby hill, known as 'Durgam'[24], which was of natural strength and on the top of which there was a retreat residence for the Palegar. When Durgam was also surrounded by the armies with their canon, the Palegar descended the hill under the cover of darkness by a secret pathway and joined his other Palegar friends like, Bangari, Yedaragunta, Thumba and Naraganti. These Palegars, gave great trouble in the region and the British armies also could not easily trace them. The government also feared that the Treasury in Vellore might be attacked by the Palegars who thus were in open rebellion. At Pullur, Col. Darley ordered for the demolition of the fort, considered as the strongest of all the Chittoor Palems. Once Pullur was reduced, the other Palegars lost hope of their success against the British armies.

Col. Darley and his army moved from Pullur towards Thumba and Bangari Palems. As the Palegars have deserted their places, their forts also were reduce to the ground. The Palegar of Bangari was an elderly man of eighty years and when the Palegars made an open rebellion, he disapproved of their acts and retired to the neighboring Cuddapah District. But his eldest son, who was the Palegar of Yedaragunta, contrary to his father, joined the other rebels in their fight against the British.

On September 19, 1804, the Nagapatla Palem was attacked by the British forces. The Palegar was aided by others like Kalluru, Pulicherla, and Pullur, but all of them were easily defeated. After this decisive engagement, there was no further resistance from them. Few days later, on 24 September, an attempt was made to capture Chandurkonda, a strong hill-fort but Col. Armstrong who led the contingent, was misled by his guides and as a result, the Palegar's men escaped. All the Palegars gave no definite answer to the terms of settlement proposed by the Collector, but they went to the neighboring Gurramkonda, then in Cuddapah District, to surrender to Thomas Munro, the Principal Collector there.

By the end of September, the rebel Palegars were entirely driven from their own Palems and were wandering in the jungles along with their Kattubadidars, saving themselves from the pursuit.[25] But some of their followers in groups started pillaging the villages and looting the properties. They also seized all the passes leading to the town, Tirupati with a view to plunder the pilgrims visiting the temple. Some of the men of Mogarala and Pakala who were active in such operations, attacked a party of government troops stationed at Mogarala and even killed five sepoys. So daring and valiant were the Palegar's men that the government thought it was necessary to protect both Tirupati and Tirumala from the rebellious Kattubadi peons of the Palem. It was also rumored that the rebel Palegars were planning to attack the temple itself.[26] Immediately the Collector, raised a body of 150 peons for ten days, to safeguard the roads leading to the temple town. Another five hundred peons were also recruited and sent to the neighboring villages in the unsettled parts of the Palems.

By this time, all the fortresses of the Palems were destroyed and the Palegars themselves were made to wander, though their followers still gave trouble to the British armies. To contain their incursions, few army posts were also set up. In order to end the rebellions, the government also announced cash rewards of one thousand Pagodas for those who apprehended a Palegar and half of that sum for those who provided information leading to their capture.[27]

## Appointment of Commission

The government of Madras, with a view to settle the affairs of the Palegars and to end the uncertainty in the collection of rents, appointed a three member Commission with Messers. Webb, Hurdis and Stratton. The last was the first Collector of the District and the predecessor of Cockburn.[28] The members of the Commission reached Chittoor on 6th. October and at once directed the Collector to suspend all the measures against pursuing the rebellious Palegars. So the military was withdrawn from all the Palems. Yet, the whereabouts of the Palegars were not known. They were constantly on the move, misleading the army through false rumors. The attempts of the army to pursue the Palegars in the Bangari jungles only resulted in their raids against the numerous villages in the plains and pillaging them. Therefore the Commissioners thought of other alternatives.

## Constructive Work of the Commission

On the suggestion of the Commission, apart from destroying all the fortifications and battlements in the Palems, several roads were taken to open up the interiors of the remote areas. A broad road from Naragallu to Chittoor was laid; this was later extended up to Vellore. Another road between Paradarami and Venkatagiri was also laid in the Yedaragunta and Bangari Palems.

Before the special Commissioners arrived in Chittoor, some of the rebel Palegars did show some signs to submit. Pulicherla Palegar for example wrote to Col. Darley, that he was willing to surrender on the condition that the Colonel sends a letter assuring his safe conduct. The Kalluru Palegar also sent a similar letter through a Vakil of the Zamindar of Punganur.[29]

The Commissioners, therefore tried few reconciliatory tactics. Mr. Webb and his co adjudicators decided to set free both the Mogarala and Pakala Palegars kept captive in Chengalpattu fort. This enabled many other Palegars to gain confidence and come to Chittoor. The Gudipati Palegar was the first to arrive and by 24 October, 1804, all other Palegars also followed and met the Commissioners. The Palegars of Naraganti, Pullur, Yedaragunta, Kalluru and Thumba attended. But Bangari was represented by his son, the Yedaragunta Palegar. These Palegars had also brought their armed peons who were more than five thousand.

The Palegars were called upon by the Commissioners to sign an agreement with the following terms:

1. They should disband their armies within one month.
2. Should destroy all the remaining fortifications and military establishments; and should desist from constructing any new ones.
3. Should assist the government in opening up the jungles by constructing roads.
4. Should pay their arrears in full by 15 December (1804), failing which they should assign their Palems to the government until the dues were fully paid.
5. They should agree to a survey of their estates and the settlement of the Peishcush of two fifths of the value of the Palem.
6. Should in future lead orderly lives and obey the orders of the government in every respect.[30]

The Palegars of Pakala, Mogarala and Thumba signed the agreement, but others evaded as they were not obviously willing to surrender their privileges for which they were traditionally accustomed. The Commissioners were surprised at the frivolous excuses the Palegars gave while rejecting the terms. Pullur Palegar sent word that he was busy in his hunting expedition, the Kalluru Palegar pretended illness, Yedaragunta also gave some lame excuse. Even Gudipati, who hitherto was considered as 'loyal' rejected the harsh terms of the Commissioners.

## Decision to deploy Army

Even before the Commissioners could recover from the surprises caused by the behavior of the Palegars, they learnt that the Pakala and Mogarala chiefs have joined with their armies the other Palegars like Kalluru, Pullur, Yedaragunta and Thumba; and were preparing to raise their banner of revolt. After waiting for two days expecting the Palegars would return for talks, the Commissioners decided to press the military to act. The Commissioners reported to the government of Madras that they were convinced that the Palegars were in no mood to come to order and that all their attempts for conciliation have proved vain. They immediately summoned three companies of sepoys from Nangamangalam, where Col. Darley had retired earlier to enable the Palegars to surrender.

## Martial Law Imposed

The government, on the Commissioners' recommendation, thought that active measures have to be adopted against the Palegars and sent a detachment of troops to Chittoor under the command of Lt. Col. Moneypenny. It consisted of an army of 3000 with artillery and cavalry. Martial law was proclaimed as the first step in dealing with the Palegars and their armies. On his arrival in Chittoor before taking the field, Moneypenny issued a proclamation asking all the rebel Palegars to submit within seven days. This did not apply to Gudipati and Naraganti, as by then they did not join the rebels in deserting the Commissioners.

The terms offered by Moneypenny were accepted by the Palegars of Bangari and Thumba, while Kalluru and Pulicherla Palegars surrendered to Thomas Munro in the Ceded Districts. But Pakala and Mogarala decided to continue their fight against the British. So the detachment marched towards Mogarala where the rebels have taken up position near a hill. On the arrival of the British forces, the armies of Mogarala withdrew during the night and crossed over to Cuddapah District only to surrender before Munro, on receiving an assurance of life and liberty.

After coming to know of the certainty of an engagement at Mogarala, the Pullur Palegar wanted to assist his friends there. But by the time he reached the hill where the armies were stationed, the allies have already moved away. He caused a considerable trouble by plundering the villages. But when the British armies closely pursued, he crossed over to Cuddapah and like the other Palegars, surrendered to Thomas Munro.

It is to be noted that the rebellious Chittoor Palegars, who decided to defy the Company authority, refused to surrender to the officer commanding the troops set against them, rejected the offers of government Commissioners and even declined to meet the special Commissioner citing some frivolous reasons. But their confidence in Thomas Munro, the Principal Collector of the neighboring Ceded districts was so high that they went to him, accepted his terms and accompanied him to be handed over to Col. Moneypenny, the officer who was commanding the troops against them in Chittoor.[31]

## Defeat of Yedaragunta Palegar

The only Palegar now left was the Yedaragunta Palegar, who proved to be more daring among all the rebels. He was joined by the dispossessed Palegar of Charagal in the neighboring Palamaner Taluk that fell in the Mysore territory.[32] To counter the allied forces of Yedaragunta and Charagal, a reinforcement was summoned from Mysore under the command of Capt. Little to assist Col. Moneypenny. Another force of one thousand irregulars were also temporarily recruited to penetrate into the jungles. The rebels made few attacks on the Mysore forces but were repulsed. The forts of Charagal as well as Yedaragunta were attacked, occupied and destroyed. The Palegars disbanded their troops and escaped into the nearby jungles. But after a hot chase, they were captured and both the Palegars were hanged.[33]

On February 8, 1805 Cockburn the Collector reported to the government that Chittoor Palems at last have been reduced to "perfect quiet". Marshal law was suspended and the military was recalled. However, Lt. Col. Darley was asked to remain for some time to preserve peace.

## Palems Forfeited

With the merciless hanging of Yedaragunta Palegar, the Revolt of Chittoor Palegars virtually came to an end. The Collector went ahead in declaring that Pakala, Mogarala, Pullur and Yedaragunta Palems as forfeited to the government. The surviving chiefs were asked to reside in Madras. The others were granted an allowance of 18 percent on the revenues of their Palems, as calculated by George Stratton, the first Collector. It was also made clear that the idea of the government was to restore those Palegars as mere revenue collectors, with permanent sannads, after due survey and assessments were carried out.[34]

The restored Palegars were allowed to collect only the land revenue and all the other taxes were left to the care of the District Collector. The Palegars continued with their Palems exercising some authority over the rural peasantry till the early part of the 20$^{th}$. century and thereafter gradually waned away. The only Palegar who could prosper was the Bangari, who later was elevated as the Zamindar and was conferred with a Sannad on an annual payment of Rs. 13,000 as Peishcush, by the Governor of Madras.[35]

The protracted revolt of the Chittoor Palegars was a valiant and concerted act of the native Chiefs against the land revenue policies adopted by the Company administration much against their interests and the way the Nawab of Arcot to whom they owed their allegiance was summarily removed. Though they were not successful in wresting their power, they made the British realize the influence they exerted on the rural peasants. The revolt also underlined the need to lay new roads and open up the jungles in the Palems which in turn helped to restore law and order.

## References

1. C.U. Aitchison, *A Collection of Treaties and Engagements and Sannads Relating t India and neighboring Countries,* Vol. V, Calcutta, p. 57
2. Though Vellore was the biggest and most populous town in the District, Chittoor was chosen as the head quarters for the reason that there were Palegars in the region who were known to be turbulent. This was proved by the fact that within 3 years of British occupation, the Palegars of Chittoor rose in revolt in 1804. However, on 1 April, 1911, when a new Chittoor District was formed with the transfer of some taluks of Cuddapah, Vellore was made as the headquarters for the North Arcot District. See for details, K.S.S. Seshan, "One Hundred Years of Chittoor District", *The Hindu, Friday Review,* (Hyderabad), 1 April, 2011, p. II.
3. The 13 Taluks were as follows: Chittoor, Chandragiri, Cuddapanatham, Tiruvallam, Kaveripak, Sholinghur, Arcot, Vellore Tiruvottiyur, Polur, Wandiwash, and Sathyaved. Arthur. F. Cox, *A Manual of the North Arcot District, in the Madras Presidency,* Madras, 1881, p. 2.
4. S. Sundararaja Iyengar, *Land Tenures in the Madras Presidency*, Madras, 1933, p. 85.
5. David Cockburn, the Collector of North Arcot District, to the Commissioners appointed to settle the affairs of the Chittoor Palems, Dated, 6 October, 1804, in *District Records, North Arcot,* (T.N. Archives) Vol. 6. p. 133.
6. K. Rajayyan, *Administration And Society in the Carnatic, 1701-1801* Sri Venkateswara University Publication, Tirupati, 1966, pp. 59-60.
7. Nilmani Mukherjee, *The Ryotwari System in Madras*, 1792- 1827, Calcutta, 1962, p. 54.
8. George Stratton's Report, in *Revenue Consultations*. Vol. 139, Paras, 4240-4262.
9. George Stratton's Report, to the Board of Revenue, fort St. George, dated 15 November, 1802, in *Revenue Consultations*, Vol. 139, p. 4321-30
10. Thomas Munro introduced in the Ceded Districts (1800-1807) the Ryotwari Settlement on a regular basis with survey and assessment of

each and every land parceled on rectangular way. For details about Thomas Munro's settlement, see, Nilmani Mukherjee, *The Ryotwari System in Madras, Op.cit.* p. 56. Also see, Burton Stein, *Thomas Munro: The Origins of the Colonial State and His Vision of Empire,* OUP, Delhi, 1989, pp.99-103

11. A. F. Cox, *op.cit,* p. 76.
12. D. Subramanyam Reddy, "Freedom Movement in Rayalaseema", *Sri Venkateswara University Golden Jubilee Souvenir,* Tirupati, 2005, p. 123.
13. A.F. Cox, *op.cit*, p. 76.
14. It may be recalled that during Uyyalawada Narasimha Reddy revolt in 1846, his first violent act was the attack on the Taluka Treasury at Koilkuntla. Treasury was considered more as symbol of the British authority and any violation of its secure position, was naturally perceived as an act of valor and challenge.
15. Stratton was told that when they started to Chittoor, one of their party tripped and fell to the ground. This was considered as a bad omen, and the attempt to go against the treasury was dropped. There were several omens followed by the people during that time. See, K. Rajayyan, *Administration And Society in The Carnatic,* Tirupati, 1966, p. 147 However, the attack on Uttanthangal was carried out. A.F. Cox, *Op.cit*, p. 76.
16. C.F. Cox, *op.cit,* 76.
17. The circular letter was sent to all the Palegars except the Palegar of Gudipati for he was by then had no dues. However, soon he also refused to clear the dues and thus joined the rebel Palegars. A.F. Cox, *Op.cit,* p. 77.
18. Taking Physic was the 'Castor- oil ceremony' that is observed periodically to cleanse the bowels. It is generally observed in the south Indian homes even today.
19. The terms of Cockburn, the Collector of North Arcot District, on 20 July, 1804, in D. Subramanyam Reddy, "The Freedom Movements in Rayalaseema", *Golden Jubilee Souvenir,* Sri Venkateswara University, Tirupati, 2005, p. 124.
20. The Mogarala Palegar also administered the affairs of Pakala as its Palegar was a minor and also a relative. See, A.F. Cox, *Op.cit*, p. 77.
21. Cockburn, the Collector of North Arcot, to the Commissioners appointed to Settle the Affairs of the Chittoor Pollams 6 October, 1804, in *North Arcot District Records*, Vol. VI, pp. 133-148.
22. *Ibid.*

23. *Ibid,* p. 78.
24. '*Durgam*' literally means, impregnable ; its steep precipice was but a natural protection for the Pullur Palegar. He had a comfortable hideout to where he withdrew during emergencies. The ruins of the buildings, and battlements ; also an open well are seen even today. For details, K.S.S. Seshan, "Chittoor Palegarla Viplawamu", Tel., *Telugu,* Quarterly Telugu Akademy Publication, Hyderabad, (April- June, 1977,) pp. 273-281.
25. Kattubadi, literally means 'Settlement'. It was used to denote land granted on favorable terms by the Palegars to their armed servants. S. Sundararaja Iyengar, *Land Tenures in the Madras Presidency,* Madras, 1933, p. 140.
26. The temple of Balaji on the Tirumala hills, considered as the richest temple in the country receives heavy amounts as "Hundi Collections". During the rule of Mohammad Ali, the Nawab of Carnatic, his brother Abdul Wahab, as the Khilladar of Chittoor, used to go to Tirumala and loot the Hundi, every weekend. However, he was defeated by Hyder Ali of Mysore and taken as a prisoner. See, K.S.S. Seshan, "Hyder Ali and his contacts With Chittoor", *Proceedings of the Andhra Pradesh History Congress, Thirteenth Session* Srisailam, 1989, p. 244.
27. Some of the Palegars thus captured were, after a nominal trial were executed in the Vellore Jail later. A. Rangarajan, "When the Vellore Sepoys rebelled" *The Hindu (Sunday Magazine Section)* Madras, August 6, 2006, p. 4.
28. The government, in its order dated, 22 September 1804 appointed the Commission to find a possible early solution to end the impasse, created on account of the rebellions of the Palegars. See, Arthur F. Cox, *Op.cit,* p. 79.
29. Punganur, in the present Chittoor District was under Cuddapah and Munro treated the Punganur Zamindari well for the kind of help the chief rendered to the English during their fight against Tipu Sultan of Mysore. For a detailed study of the Punganur relations with the British, see, K.S.S. Seshan, *British Role in Rural Economy,* New Delhi, 1989, pp. 15-16.

30 Terms and conditions of the Commissioners to the Chittoor Palegars, Chittoor, Dt. 24 October, 1804, in A.F. Cox, *A Manual of North Arcot District,* Madras, 1881, p. 79.

31 T.H. Beaglehole, *Thomas Munro: And the Development of Administrative Policy in Madras*, 1792- 1818, CUP. 1966, p. 68.

32. Charagal Palegar when revolted against the British, he was imprisoned by the Collector of Krishnagiri, Col. Reid, and his Palem was taken over. However, in 1794, he escaped from the prison and became a vagabond. When the Chittoor Palegars revolted in 1800, he decided to jump into the fray and help Yedaragunta Palegar. He even commanded a contingent of Yedaragunta Kattubadi forces and plundered several Villages in the Krishnagiri District, then in Mysore. See for details, Divireddy Subramanyam Reddy, "Freedom Movements in Rayalaseema", *S.V. University Golden Jubilee* Vol. *Op.cit*, p. 128.
33. A.F. Cox, *Op.cit*, p. 81.
34. The survey and classification of the entire Chittoor District was carried in 1805, and the accounts known as 'Paimash' were prepared. These accounts became the basis for all the future assessments. Devireddy, op.cit. p. 129.
35. K.S.S. Seshan, "Banaripalem Zamindars" *Vaartha*, Telugu, Chittoor edition, 1 April, 2011.

## Chapter - VIII

# Wahabi Conspiracy: Revolt of Rasool Khan (1839)

One of the important rebellions against the English in Andhra in the first half of the $19^{th}$ century was that of Rasool Khan, the Nawab of Kurnool. The rebellion which occurred in 1839 was a part of the Wahabi movement which at that time swept across the country. In the Deccan, Prince, Mubarez-ud-Doulah, the younger brother of the Nizam of Hyderabad was the central figure of the Wahabi movement and along with several other chiefs, he is construed to have made a concerted effort against the presence of the British. The Kurnool Nawab's anti – British sentiment was so strong that he became a close confident of the Hyderabad Prince and rose the banner of revolt against the Company administration. [1]

Gulam Rasool Khan, at the instance of Mubarez-ud- Doulah, set up an armory and in utmost secrecy, manufactured arms and ammunition on an unprecedented scale to help the rebels with the sole aim of driving the British away from the country. But as ill-luck would have it, before he could strike, the British were able to unearth the conspiracy through their intelligence agencies and the Nawab's attempts were foiled. Though he was defeated in the battle, imprisoned and supposedly got killed, his determination to oust the British rule and the sacrifice he made served as an inspiring example for the posterity. He gave his life for the cause of ridding the foreign yoke at a time when the very idea to oppose the mighty British authority was in a nascent stage.

## Rise of Kurnool Nawabs

After the defeat and destruction of the Vijayanagar empire in the battle of Tallikota in 1565, several tributaries in the Deccan and South India declared their independence. The remaining part of the kingdom of the Vijayanagar was divided between the victors. The territory of Kurnool along with Adoni and Nandyal went as the share to the Nawab of Bijapur; while Golconda obtained Ongole and Kondaveedu (Guntur). The Kurnool territory was held by one Gopal Raju, a grandson of Alia Rama Raju, the 90 year old Vijayanagar commander, who was killed in the battle of Tallikota.[2] When the Nawab of Bijapur, Adil Shah sent his commander Abdul Wahab to take control of Kurnool, Gopal Raju resisted the forces of Bijapur, but was overpowered by the Nawab's armies and Kurnool came under the rule of Bijapur. Adoni and Nandyal fell to Abdul Wahab with no resistance. Abdul Wahab held these territories as a deputy of the Bijapur Sultan almost up to 1618 A.D.

There was in Kurnool by then a strong fort and also the iconic Kondareddy buruz. But Wahab strengthened the fortifications, beautified the palace with large gateways and several bastions around the fort.[3] But during the period of Aurangzeb, the Mughal emperor, Bijapur along with other Deccani kingdoms like Golconda were defeated and the territories were placed under a commander, Ghiyas –ud- din[4]. But after some time, as Ghias-ud-din was not popular, the Mughal emperor appointed Dawood Khan Patan in the place of Ghias. The new chief was also bestowed the title, "Nawab". Dawood Khan ruled Kurnool from 1690 to 1715.

After the death of Nawab Dawood Khan, his brother Ibrahim Khan succeeded as the Nawab of Kurnool. Ibrahim Khan had two sons and the younger one, Alaf Khan accepted the suzerainty of the Nizam, Asaf Jah I and was recognized as the Nawab of Kurnool.[5] Alaf Khan ruled up to 1733 and was succeeded by his son, Himayat Khan. The new Nawab played a decisive role in the affairs of the Deccan during the crucial Carnatic Wars when Nasir Jung and Muzzafar Jung were fighting for the succession at Hyderabad after the death of Nizam –ul-Mulk. After Himayat Khan, his son, Rahmath Khan succeeded as the Nawab and he had a long reign of nearly 40 years. During his period, Kurnool was taken over by Hyder Ali of Mysore and the Nawab agreed to pay an annual tribute of Rs. two Lakhs.

In 1792, after the death of Rahmath Khan, his son, Alaf Khan succeeded to the throne. It was during his period that the Ceded Districts were acquired by the British and Thomas Munro was appointed as the Principal Collector.[6] After the death of Alaf Khan in 1815, his first son Munwar Khan became the Nawab. In 1823, when Munwar passed away, his younger brother Gulam Rasool Khan came to the throne. It was this Rasool Khan who was drawn to the Wahabi movement, rose in revolt against the British in 1839 and thus became a martyr for the cause of anti-British struggle.

## Gulam Rasool Khan: (1805-1839)

Rasool Khan, born in 1805 was the last of the six sons of Alaf Khan, the Nawab of Kurnool (1792-1815). But he was the most favorite of the father.[7] As an young boy, Rasool was taught Arabic, Urdu and Telugu by tutors in the Palace itself. He was also well trained in martial arts. He excelled in horse-riding, sword fighting and in the use of fire arms. He was also taught Islamic religious texts. He was shrewd, intelligent and very humane. Alaf Khan was of the opinion that after him, though youngest of his sons, Rasool alone was suitable for succession.[8]

Alaf Khan died in 1815 at the age of 65. The Diwan, Nawaz Khan, in consultation with other nobles like, Miandari Khan,[9] in order not to incur the displeasure of the followers of the eldest son, declared Munnawar as the successor to Alaf Khan. Munnawar had a rule for eight years and at the age of 50 he died in 1823. He was succeeded by his brother, Rasool Khan who by then was 18 years and thus had come of age.[10] Like many other native rulers, Rasool Khan also had an in born hatred for the presence of the English in India. He decided to stand solidly against the alien rule. The anti-British stand that Rasool Khan took was also due to his close association with the Wahabi movement, which at that time was spreading all over the country.

## Wahabi Movement and Its Work

With a view to see that the basic tenets of Islam are followed strictly and with sincerity, there arose in the 17th.century a reform movement, popularly known as Wahabi Movement. The movement was started by one Wahab (1691-1787) and therefore it was named after him. The main objective of the movement was to impress on the rulers to keep the welfare of the people as their primary duty in governance. But over a period of time, the movement also had undergone changes in its aims and objectives. Wahabi movement was popularized in India by two Islamic religious leaders: Shahwaliullah (1703-1762) and his able son, Abdul Aziz (1746-1823). Both of them toured several places in North India for the spread of the Wahabi movement.

But the most effective work for the spread of Wahabi movement in India was carried by Syed Ahmed Bareilly[11]. Syed Ahmed, early in life, joined the army under one, Amir Khan and acquired all the military skills. He was attracted to the Wahabi movement and with a view to understand the intricacies of the movement, he went to Mecca. He came to the conclusion that if India wanted to become free from foreign rule, the only hope was the Wahabi movement. After his return to India, Syed Ahmed Bareilly decided to work for the spread of the Wahabi movement.

By 1820, Wahabi movement spread from Bengal to North Western Frontier Province (NWFP) and from United Provinces to Madras in South. The main stronghold for Wahabis was Patna. Bareilly toured the entire length and breadth of the country and addressed large gatherings. Wherever he went, he exhorted people to oppose the colonial masters who were exploiting the nation. His message was that everyone should rise above the religious considerations to oppose the alien rule. He gave the slogan, *"Jan ko denge- vathan ko bachayenge"*[12]. (Let us sacrifice our lives; but safeguard our motherland"). It was on account of his tireless work that Wahabi movement became widespread.

## Rasool Khan and the Wahabi Movement

Gulam Rasool Khan, the Nawab of Kurnool, came under the influence of the Wahabi movement, which found great patronage in Mubarez –ud –Doulah, the younger brother of Nasir-ud- Doulah, the Nizam of Hyderabad.[13] As the movement preached for social reform and political advancement among the Muslims, Rasool Khan also was attracted towards the movement at the behest of Mubarez –ud-Doulah.

With a view to counter the British, Rasool Khan took steps to reform his army. A separate contingent, with Arab Rohillas known for their fighting spirit was recruited with modern weaponry. He also modernized the administrative set up . He replaced several of the earlier officers with able men of character and ability.[14]

When Mubarez –ud –Doulah came to know of the independent nature of Rasool Khan and his opposition to the British, he sent his men to strike a secret alliance with the Nawab of Kurnool. The followers of Mubarez made it possible for the Hyderabad prince and the Nawab of Kurnool to come to an understanding and work for the success of the Wahabi movement[15]. As per the request of Mubarez, Rasool Khan agreed to establish a secret arsenal to manufacture arms and ammunition that was needed for any concerted insurrection which they contemplated. Mubarez, on his part assured of monetary help for the manufacture of such arms[16].

Syed Ahmed Bairelli died in the year 1831 but his followers kept up the Wahabi movement and anti-British agitation throughout India for a number of years.[17] Two of his close followers, Moulavi Vilayat Ali and Salim came to the Deccan in 1838. A number of their agents were working in places like Madras, Bangalore, Kurnool and Bombay. In Hyderabad, Mubarez has become the centre of the Wahabi insurrections. Besides other chiefs, the Nawab of Kurnool also was confided by the Wahabi agents. The activities of the Wahabis greatly increased when it was widely believed that the Russian troops were advancing from Central Asia towards India.[18]

Rasool Khan recruited a band of committed young activists who in the guise of fakirs and religious mendicants started visiting even remote places for the spread of Wahabi movement. He gave utmost importance to the establishment of an arsenal as requested by Mubarez-ud-Doulah. An underground arms manufacturing unit was established in the Palace gardens outside the Fort in Kurnool. There was also a foundry set up to cast Canons of high caliber. Utmost secrecy was maintained in running these underground establishments. In the arsenals, swords ,knives, daggers, guns, pistols of various sizes, and gun- powder etc. were manufactured. The arms and ammunition thus manufactured were stored in underground structures built for the purpose in and outside of the fort. In the Begam Bagh, adjacent to the fort, there were few such cellars where thousands of guns and gunpowder were concealed. They were all meant to be sent out to the youth for use whenever a rebellion was declared. It was also the intention of the Nawab to equip the youngsters working for the Wahabi movement, with proper arms.

Enthused by the progress that the Nawab of Kurnool was making, Mubarez –ud-Doulah contemplated of a personal visit to Kurnool to see for himself how well the entire preparations were being carried.[19] It was the plan of the Wahabis that "Mubarez will take command of the combined armies at Kurnool and after overthrowing the British, through insurrection, he would crown himself as the Nizam of Hyderabad in the place of his brother, Nasir –ud-Doulah".[20]

## Role of Mubarez -ud-Doulah

As the Prince of Hyderabad with greater access to wealth and having a private army of more than a lakh, Mubarez devoted all his time and resources for the Wahabi movement and the anti-British activities from a very young age.[21] The revolt of Rasool Khan of Kurnool is intimately connected to the Wahabi movement and the anti-British activities of Mubarez-ud-Doulah. Moreover, the entire conspiracy of Rasool Khan came to light when Mubarez's role was enquired into. Hence a brief account of the role played by Mubarez becomes necessary in this study.

Mubarez –ud-Doulah was born in 1800 and thus was almost of the same age as that of Rasool Khan of Kurnool. He was the younger brother of Nasir-ud-Doulah, Asaf Jah III, the Nizam of Hyderabad (1829- 1857 ).[22] Mubarez, as a boy, had good education in Persian, Arabic and his grounding in religion was also sound. He had an independent spirit from his boyhood. Mubarez developed hatred towards the English from the beginning. Even in his father's reign, he had shown a rebellious spirit and dislike for the presence of the British power in Hyderabad. As a result he was imprisoned for nearly five years (1815-1820) by his own father, Sikandar Jah.[23]

Mubarez –ud-Doulah had another phase of incarceration, but this time during the period of his brother, Nasir-ud-Doulah. In 1830, Mubarez collected a large body of Arabs and Afghans, strengthened his garrison around his palace in the city and started an insurrection against the British. Then a contingent of troops under Col. Stewart marched against Mubarez and arrested him. The prince, as per the desire of Nizam, was sent to the fort of Golconda and imprisoned on 19 April, 1830. After few months, he was released and returned to his palace in the city. The insurrection of Mubarez against the British and his arrest by Col. Stewart are graphically recounted by Col. Meadows Taylor, in his book, "The Story Of my Life".[24] Mubarez was known among the British residents in Hyderabad as "obstinate, had rebellious spirit and strong will power."[25] The hatred of Mubarez-ud-Doulah towards the British, even when he was an young boy was such that once his father Sikandar Jah wanted a sentry of a British army to be posted as a guard at his palace. But the young boy replied that he would prefer to die rather than to see a British guard at his palace gate.[26] Thus Mubarez's animosity for the British was well known. When he came to know of the Wahabi movement and its avowed opposition to the British rule in India, he decided to work for its success.

## Mubarez's Designs

Gen. Fraser, the British Resident at Hyderabad, as soon as he came to know of the Wahabi activities and the suspected involvement of Mubarez –ud Doulah, ordered for a strict watch on the activities of the Prince. Fraser came to know through his intelligent agents that Mubarez was carrying out correspondence with several persons in and out of the state. There were about 20 thousand Wahabi followers in the city of Hyderabad alone. The disaffected chiefs of Hindustan were trying to unite with their forces against the English and recognize the suzerainty of the Shah of Persia. Wahabis in India believed that the Shah would appoint

Mubarez –ud-Doulah as the Subedar of the Deccan after driving away the British and deposing the Nizam, Nasir –ud Doulah. With that strong belief, Mubarez started sending his emissaries to several places like Lahore, Sindh, Gwalior, Bombay, Kurnool, Madras, Sholapur etc. He also secretly got a seal made with an imposing title, "Raisul Muslimin"[27] The Resident also came to know of the "hostile intentions of Mubarez" against the British government to convert the native troops at Secunderabad and Nagpur for the cause of the Wahabi movement.

Gen. Fraser after being convinced that the activities of Mubarez were detrimental to the British administration, spoke to the Nizam, Nasir –ud-Doulah and convinced him of the conspiracy that was being attempted by his brother against both the British as well as the government of the Nizam. Immediately, Mubarez-ud –Doulah was taken into custody and was put under guards in the fort of Golconda.[28] All his close associates who were involved in the spread of Wahabi movement, numbering 46 were also captured and imprisoned.[29]

## Judicial Enquiry Commission

The Resident, Col. Fraser wanted to institute a Judicial enquiry into the Wahabi conspiracy on behalf of the government of the Company as well as the government of the Nizam as the offence was targeted against both the governments. Accordingly the government constituted a Commission of Enquiry consisting of 6 members; three were nominated by the Resident and the other three were the nominees of the Nizam's administration.[30]

The Commission sat in sessions from 28 June 1839 to March 1840. Through its sittings, the Commission found that Mubarez was engaged in a conspiracy with the Nawab of Kurnool and also was in secret alliance with a number of other chiefs like the Nawab of Tonk, the Nawab of Rampur, and several others with a view to overthrow the Nizam and declare himself as the ruler and also to bring an insurrection against the British. The Enquiry Commission also felt that Mubarez tried with his close associates to spread sedition among the Muslim sepoys stationed in Secunderabad. [31]

As a result of the findings of the Commission, Mubarez-ud-Doulah had to spend the rest of his life as a state prisoner in the Golconda fort and died on 25th June 1854.[32]

## Network of Spies

The Enquiry Commission and its work becomes central to the unearthing of the contemplated insurrection of the Nawab of Kurnool. As the entire conspiracy by the Nawab of Kurnool was planned with utmost secrecy, it would not have come to the notice of the British if there was no rigorous enquiry into the affairs of Mubarez and his men in Hyderabad. The Enquiry Commission, in its work had come across the active role of spies in the service of the Mubarez- ud-Doulah through whom Mubarez carried correspondence pertaining to the proposed Wahabi insurrection.

The spies and couriers who joined Mubarez were paid a monthly allowance between Rs. 12 to Rs. 100 a month.[33] The 46 Maulvis who were arrested when the conspiracy busted, were all found to be acting as spies and couriers for Mubarez. Of them, ten were categorized as the key players in the entire episode. Through their depositions before the Commission as the key witnesses, the activities of Mubarez as well as the Wahabis came to light. It was also found through these spies, that Mubarez was in close touch with the native princes like Satara, Baroda, Rohilkhand, Bhopal, Jodhpur, Patiala etc. who all have expressed their willingness to support him against the British.[34] But the most important one with whom Mubarez was in league was the Nawab of Kurnool. In the interrogation, it was revealed that Maulvi Salim, a close associate of Mubarez, used to write and receive letters from the Nawab of Kurnool on behalf of Mubarez. Once, Mubarez on being told that there was a letter from the Nawab of Kurnool, he instructed Salim to write to Rasool Khan that "I will also come out within a fortnight. He (Rasool Khan) need not worry."[35] One witness revealed that he saw Imam Khan, another confidant of Mubarez had kept letters in his turban and as a courier he had just then returned from Kurnool after meeting the Nawab there.[36] Imam Khan, himself in his deposition revealed that Mubarez and the Nawab of Kurnool were "good friends". Abdul Razak was arrested in Nellore and he was in possession of a letter written by the Sheriff of Mecca to the Nawab of Kurnool. A letter recovered in the palace of Mubarez revealed that if Mubarez were to be successful (in his rebellion) a high post was assured to the Kurnool Nawab. Maulvi Shuja ud din, another Maulvi, was a trusted follower of Mubarez and he was a great admirer of the Nawab of Kurnool.

Mubarez also used the spies to send besides letters, even money to the chiefs. The spies were paid according to the nature of the work they were entrusted with. The chief of Udgir was a follower of Mubarez and "a good Musalman". Mubarez had sent him a lakh of rupees to store the needed grain, arms and ammunition.[37]

Regarding the unity and cooperation between Mubarez –ud-Doulah and Rasool Khan of Kurnool, there were several evidences for the enquiry commission. There was a letter dated, 23 August,1839, brought to the Resident, Col. Fraser by the brother of the Nawab of Kurnool, purported to have been written secretly by the Nawab to Mubarez.[38] There was yet another episode of a letter written by Mubarez to the Nawab of Kurnool that was intercepted by the British agents. Mubarez in that letter had spelled out his plans for the final assault on the British requesting him to "dispatch the needed arms for such an attack". If only this letter has reached the Nawab, and had he acted. The Enquiry Commission felt that the results would have been very "disastrous".[39]

## Attack on Rasool Khan (1839)

What is significant in the Enquiry Commission's work was the unearthing of the role that Kurnool Nawab played in the anti-British campaign, his close links with Mubarez and above all establishing an armory with a view to overthrow the British authority. On the reports from the Resident of Hyderabad, the government of Madras immediately decided to act against the Nawab of Kurnool.

As Kurnool was in the jurisdiction of the Ceded Districts and under the control of the Company administration in Madras, the government based on the reports of the Resident at Hyderabad, brought the following charges against the Nawab of Kurnool.

(i) That he (Rasool Khan) caused disaffection, of harboring designs hostile to the British power and its allies, of augmentation of his military establishments; of the repairs for his fortifications and of secret accumulation of military stores.

(ii) Charges of acts of violence, tyranny and maladministration of the country, of inflicting injuries on the British subjects and of indifference to demands for reparation made thereof.[40]

To investigate into the above charges, the British government sent an enquiry Commission to Kurnool, consisting of T.L. Blane, of the Madras Civil Service and Col. S.W. Steel, the Military Secretary to Government. A military contingent under the command of Col. Dyce was dispatched from Bellary to "render assistance to the Commission if need be".[41] The government of Madras also instructed Col. Fraser, the Resident at Hyderabad to dispatch another body of troops to Kurnool in addition to the troops from Bellary. It was then the Resident, as already pointed out, asked Col. Armstrong, to proceed with his contingent to assist Col. Dice and his army against the Nawab of Kurnool.[42]

At that time, Armstrong was engaged as the President of the Judicial Commission that was enquiring into the Wahabi conspiracy by Mubarez in Hyderabad. The work of the Commission was stopped for a while because Armstrong was asked to proceed to Kurnool. The following note in the proceedings of the Enquiry Commission reveals the action initiated against Kurnool:

> The sittings of the Commission was suspended from 4 August 1839 to 21 January, 1840 due to the absence of Armstrong as he was asked to proceed against Kurnool Nawab. The sittings were further postponed due to the delay in the return of Armstrong as he was busy with Captain Malcolm in Kurnool, in investigating the papers which were discovered there, and they were crucial to the trial of Mubarez-ud-Doulah.[43]

The members of the Commission under T.L. Blane along with the military contingents, arrived at Kurnool on 12 September, 1839. They held a series of meetings extending for about a month with the Diwan and the brother of the Nawab. But as no information was forthcoming, the Commissioners decided to search the Nawab's fort and the Palace for which the Nawab refused. But under the threat of the Commission, Rasool Khan vacated the fort, sent all the women folk to safety and with his army proceeded to *Johrapur*, a village, about a mile from the fort. There, he took shelter at the Dargah of Hazrath Sayed Ahmed Shah Quadri, with his Arab and Rohilla troops guarding him[44].

The Commission then entered the fort and unearthed the huge accumulation of arms and ammunition stored and concealed in the underground cellars. The Commission instructed on 18 October, 1839, Lt. Col. Dyce, the commandant, to proceed with the army against the Nawab who was stationed in Johrapur. The Nawab also by then fell into arrears of pay for his Rohilla and Arab troops. The combined armies of Col. Dice and Col. Armstrong surrounded Johrapur. They made an announcement for the surrender of the Nawab or else to face the consequences. But the Nawab and his commander, Shah Wali Khan decided to fight rather than surrender. The British troops opened fire and a fierce battle ensued. The Nawab's armies though resisted for a while, were defeated. There were about hundred causalities on the Nawab's side while the British lost not more than two officers and another twenty wounded. The war "lasted but for few hours", as recorded by the Commission of Enquiries at Hyderabad, in its report to the Resident.[45]

All the important commanders of the Nawab like Shah Wali Khan, Noor Khan, Sheik Sayed etc. were killed in the battle. Rasool Khan, the Nawab was captured by Major Armstrong. He was deposed and his territory was confiscated by the Company administration. The Nawab was then sent under escort to Madras and from there was deported to Trichinopalle, where he was imprisoned in the Fort there.[46] The Judicial Enquiry Commission that was set up against Mubarez -ud- Doulah, had also briefly recorded in its Report on the action taken against Kurnool thus : "The operations against the Nawab of Kurnool took place in October, 1839. After a short and sharp struggle, Kurnool surrendered and the Nawab was taken prisoner."[47]

After the capture of the Nawab, Col Armstrong and Col. Dice along with Mr. Malcolm were engaged in locating the arms stored in the secret vaults in the fort of Kurnool. They carried out digging in several places in and outside of the Fort. In the Begam Bagh area, outside of the fort, they unearthed several underground cellars where a number of swords, guns, canon, daggers, pistols and huge amounts of gun-powder was stored. Thus the charge of "secret accumulation of stores and canon on an extensive scale" was proved though, as the Enquiry Commission felt, the charge against the Nawab of "harboring designs against the government" had no clear proof.

## Kurnool Under The British

Kurnool, after its assumption by the government, was placed under the Commissioner and a military Assistant, to administer as a non-regulation province. T.L. Blane was the first Commissioner and Col. Steel, the first military Assistant. Kurnool continued to be a non-regulation Province up to 1858 when it was made as a separate District and a Collector, under the general regulations, came to be appointed.[48]

The family of Rasool Khan was sanctioned pension by the government. An annual amount of Rs. 2,22,651-4-0 was paid to the members of the family per year. But by 1886, this amount was so reduced that only an amount of Rs. 55,000 was given to the family members One of the grandsons of the Nawab, Dawood Khan was getting a personal pension of Rs 70 per month in 1890. However the daughters of the Nawab were given only life pensions.[49]

It may be mentioned here that the Jagirdar of Udayagiri in Nellore District who was an ardent follower of Gulam Rasool Khan and who also was in close correspondence with Mubarez –ud-Doulah was removed from his Jagir in 1838. The Udayagiri Jagir was sequestrated by the British "as it was proved that he participated in the Wahabi conspiracy engineered by Nawab of Kurnool against the British"[50]

## Death of Rasool Khan

After about eight months in the prison at the Trichinopalle, it was reported that the Nawab, Rasool Khan was murdered by his own servant, Yakub Khan. The government later hanged the murderer of the Nawab. The body of Rasool khan was handed over to his family members and it was buried in Kurnool, in the precincts of the Dargah of the Hazrath Moulvi Miskeen, patron saint of the family of the Nawabs.[51]

There have been a number of versions on the death of the Nawab. The widely circulated belief in and around Kurnool has been that he was poisoned to death. According to another version, the Nawab was regularly attending a Christian Chapel within the fort premises and one day while he was returning from the Chapel, his servant, a devout Muslim, assassinated the Nawab.[52].

The rebellion of Rasool Khan, is a major landmark in the anti-British movement in the early part of the 19th. century. It remains as a bright chapter in the history of the freedom struggle in the country. The saga of the life of the Nawab, Rasool Khan stand as a testimony to the independent spirit of the young Nawab who sincerely made an attempt to drive away the British with the help of other like minded chiefs like Mubarez ud Doulah. His patriotic fervor and his heroic struggle against the British remained as an inspiration for the future generations in this part of the country. Even now, the selfless and valiant struggle carried out by Rasool Khan is gratefully remembered by the people of the entire Rayalaseema region.

## References

1. K.S.S. Seshan, " Of Passion, Rebellion and Conspiracy", *The Hindu, Metro Plus,* Hyderabad, June, 11, p. 4.
2. For details on the division of the territories among the victors, aftermath of the Tallikota battle, see, Dharani Ramachandra Rao, *Kurnoolu Mandala Charithramu*, (first published 1936) Kurnool, 2001, p. 34.
3. Abdul Wahab thus could be considered as the person who laid the foundations for the establishment of a Nawabi of Kurnool. He died in Kurnool and his tomb lies close to the Handri river, known today as "Abdul Wahab Gummaz". However, he was not conferred the title, Nawab. For details, see, S.D.V. Aziz, *Gulam Rasool Khan*, Hyderabad, 2011, pp. 15-17.
4. It was Ghias-ud-din who named the town as 'Kurnool', as its earlier name was Kandenavol.
5. Quamaruddin who was appointed as the governor of the Deccan by the Mughal emperor, declared independence and proclaimed himself

as the Nizam, Asaf Jah I after defeating the Mughal representative, Mubarez khan in 1724. It is said that as a Mughal loyalist, Ibrahim of Kurnool went in support of Mubarez and was killed in the battle of Shekarkelda. See for details about this battle, Henry George Briggs, *The Nizam: His History and Relations with the British Government,* (first published, 1861) Vol. 1. Delhi, 1985, p. 31.

6. It was Thomas Munro who was appointed as the first Principal Collector of the Ceded Districts and Alaf Khan was thus contemporary to Thomas Munro.
7. The other sons like Munnawar Khan and Muzafar Khan were pleasure loving and therefore, Alaf Khan thought that Rasool Khan will make a good ruler. He even declared Rasool as his successor. Narahari Gopalakrishnama Chetty, *A Manual of The Kurnool District in The Presidency of Madras*, (Madras, 1886), pp. 50-51.
8. The first son, Munnawar was a puppet in the hands of his young wife and showed no interest for administration. The second, Muzzafar Khan was a debauch and he was given to the pleasures of palace life. Munnawar once showed signs of rebellion against his father for his open bias towards the brother, Rasool Khan for which Munnawar was even punished with imprisonment for a short period. He was released on the promise of good conduct. But as Rasool was hardly a lad of 9 years of age, Munnawar came to the throne in 1815 after the death of Alaf Khan. S.D.V. Aziz, op.cit., P.44. For a detailed description of the dynastic history of the Kurnool Nawabs, see, Dharani Ramachandra Rao, *Kurnool Mandala Charithramu*, (First published 1936) Kurnool, 2001, pp. 35-40.
9. Miandari Khan was the Financial advisor to Alaf Khan and was also his brother-in-law. When Rasool Khan became the Nawab in May, 1823, Maindari Khan was appointed as his Diwan. S.A.D. Aziz, *Ibid*. p 52. Ironically, it was this Diwan, who turned out to be a traitor when the Nawab was attacked by the British. S.A.D. Aziz, *Ibid*, p. 88. However, in some works, the name of the Diwan is stated as Namdhari Khan. See, Dharani Ramachandra Rao, *Op.cit*, p. 49.
10. The other brother, Muzzafar Khan, however, had gone in the meantime to Adoni, where he lived with his wife and children. In a fit of rage, he killed his wife and was therefore taken into custody by the British as Adoni was then under the Company administration. He was tried and imprisoned in the British jail in Bellary. The other brothers did not show much interest to claim the Nawabi. Thus Rasool Khan's succession was free from any opposition. *Ibid*. p. 46.

11. Syed Hussan Askari, "Political significance of the Movement of Syed Ahmed Brailvi" *Indian Historical Records Commission's Proceedings,* Vol. XXXI, Part II, Mysore, January, 1955, p. 180.
12. S.D.V. Aziz, *Ibid*, p. 48.
13 It may be noted that Mubarez ud- Doulah, the brother of the Nizam had impressed on Rasool Khan on the need to support Wahabi movement with a view to drive the British away. However, there are many testimonies to show that they were good friends and shared common views regarding the anti-British stand they had taken. See, K. Maddaiah, *Freedom Movement in Rayalaseema,* New Delhi, 2012, p. 47.
14 The role the spies played in the spread of the Wahabi movement is significant. Mubarez of Hyderabad had a huge contingent of spies who were dispatched to various places for the effective spread of Wahabism. Rasool Khan also gave great importance to the spies in this regard. S.D.V. Aziz, *Ibid,* p. 51.
15. *The Freedom Struggle in Hyderabad,* (A Connected Account) Published by the Hyderabad State Committee appointed for the Compilation of a History of the Freedom Movement in Hyderabad. Vol. I, 1956, p. 126.
16. At one stage, a spy sent by Mubarez to the Nawab of Kurnool was caught by the English army men. It was found that the spies were carrying letters addressed to the Nawab. This strengthens the view that Mubarez was supporting for the manufacture of arms in Kurnool. *Freedom Struggle in Hyderabad, Section 29,* p. 139.
17. Syed Ahmed died in a battle that took place on 1 May, 1831 at Balcot, while fighting against the Sikhs who were supporting the cause of the English. Several of his supporters a were also killed in the battle. S.D.V. Aziz, I*bid,* p. 63.
18. See for details, *Freedom Struggle in Hyderabad*, ibid, p. 126.
19. Mubarez also had indicated to one of his Moulvis, who had come from a visit to Kurnool, that he was planning to go there soon. There was also the testimony of Gulam Ahmed, the agent of Mubarez who reported after meeting the Nawab of Kurnool, that "Everything was settled and well planned". See for details, *The Freedom Struggle in Hyderabad,* Vol. I, Hyderabad, 1956, p. 141.
20. K. Maddaiah, *Freedom Movement in Rayalaseema,* Op.cit. p. 69.
21. Report of the Commission of Enquiry on Mubarez-ud –Doulah, Section-35, Quoted in *The Freedom Struggle in Hyderabad*, p. 127.
22. It was in his name, that Secunderabad came into being in 1805 for the stationing of the Company troops.

23. In Aug.1815 a servant of Mubarez had a quarrel with a tailor who was in the service of the British officials in Hyderabad Residency. Conflict became serious and the servant took refuge with Mubarez, who got the tailor arrested. But as the Resident Russell, got interested in the case, he sent an army with two cannons against Mubarez. His house was besieged, but Mubarez's African cavalry repulsed the attack. A soldier of the Company army was also killed in the attack and soon Russell's troops withdrew. The Resident took it as an insult and became furious. Sensing a greater trouble, the then Prime-Minister, Chandulal with a view to douse the issue, spoke to the Nizam, Sikandar Jah. Mubarez-ud-Doulah along with his close associates were kept in the Golconda fort under the surveillance of the Nizam's troops for 5 years (1815 1820). At that time, Mubarez was a lad of mere 15 years. For details of this revolt of Mubarez, see, *The Freedom Struggle in Hyderabad*, p. 120.
24. Philip Meadows Taylor was a senior officer in the British subsidiary army at Secunderabad and was a famous novelist. Taylor was the first Anglo-Indian Writer. He was known for several novels like, *Sitha*, *Confessions of a Thug, Tipu Sultan,*etc. He had married the daughter of Henry Palmer, who established the famous Hyderabad based financial concern, "Palmer & Company".
25. This was the assessment of the Commission, which enquired into the conspiracy of Mubarez, Quoted in *The Freedom Struggle in Hyderabad,* p. 163.
26. See, the Commission of Enquiry, Quoted in *The Freedom Struggle in Hyderabad*, p. 163.
27. The title meant, the supreme of all the Musalmans, was also to impress on his men that Mubarez was working for the establishment of a supreme government free from the interference of the British. See for details of the activities of Mubarez, (Section, 61 to 122) Enquiry Committee Report quoted in *The Freedom struggle in Hyderabad State*, pp. 145-153.
28. It was not easy to send Mubarez to confinement. The combined forces of the British and the Nizam were pressed into service to force him into custody. *Ibid*. p. 130.
29. Of the 46, ten of the close followers of Mubarez were identified as key persons and they were detained for a longer period while the rest were released after the Enquiry was over. The ten leaders were: Moulavi Salim;2. Lal Khan; 3. Syed Abbas; 4 Md. Asif; 5. Elahi Bakshi; 6. Abdur Razak; 7. Pir Muhammad; 8. Md. Faizullah; 9. Abdur Rahman Khan; and 10. Syed Khasim. The above leaders were key witnesses in the

enquiry and the committee gave a detailed description of their role in the conspiracy in their report. Para 17 of the preamble of the Enquiry Committee Report. Quoted in *The Freedom Struggle in Hyderabad. Op..Cit* . p. 133.

30. The members of the Commission were as follows: Col. Fraser's nominees: Major Armstrong, (President of the Commission) Capt. Hutton and Malcolm. The nominees of the Nizam were Aziz ud Doulah, Kurshid Jung and Benezar Jung. See, *The Freedom Struggle in Hyderabad, op.cit,* p. 132.
31. *Ibid.,* pp. 129-130.
32. The death of Mubarez is reported in a letter by G.A. Bushby, the Resident to the Government of India on 26 June 1854. See for the text of the letter, *Ibid*. p. 177.
33. Section 141, Enquiry Commission Report, in *The Freedom Movement in Hyderabad, op.cit*, p. 159.
34. *Ibid.*, p. 134.
35. The intention of Mubarez to visit Kurnool was to look for himself at the preparations made there. But this proposed visit unfortunately did not materialize, as he was sent to prison before embarking any such visit.
36. Report of the Enquiry Commission, Section 115, Quoted in, *The Freedom Struggle in Hyderabad*, p. 152.
37. Udgir, because of its stragical importance, (being in the centre of Carnatic,) was chosen by Mubarez to store grain. The place had a strong fort and its ruler, Abbas Ali Khan was a strong follower of the Wahabi movement. When the involvement of the Nawab of Udgir was proved, the British government confiscated the whole of his estate, and the Nawab was deported by the government. *Ibid*. Section 23, p. 139. For details of the role of Abbas Ali Khan, see, *The Freedom Struggle in Hyderabad,* p. 145.
38. It may be recalled that the sons of Munnawar Khan, were trying to have the throne of Kurnool for themselves after the death of their father in 1823.Therefore they were conspiring against Rasool Khan by intercepting his correspondence with Mubarez., *Enquiry Commission Report*. Section-104.
39. This has been a controversial letter supposed to have been written by Mubarez to Rasool Khan asking him to dispatch the arms. The courier of the letter was Muhammad Khan, a trusted follower of Mubarez. The letter was concealed in an amulet and he tried to deliver it to the Nawab of Kurnool. But as the English surveillance was very strict, fearing the capture by the British, Muhammad Khan tied the amulet to the hand

of an old beggar woman living in a sarai at Mustaidpura, where himself took shelter in the guise of a traveler. The amulet was recovered by the guards while combing the area and was duly handed over to the Resident Col. Fraser and thus the entire conspiracy came to light. This letter also brought to light beyond any doubt the role of Rasool Khan, the Nawab of Kurnool, in the seditious acts against the English. For details about this significant letter, see. S.D.V. Aziz, *Ibid*. pp. 73-74. There is also reference to the 'Armlet' in the Enquiry commission Report of Mubarez –ud –Doulah. see, Section 106, *The Freedom Struggle in Hyderabad, Op.cit,* p. 151.

40. N. Gopalakrishnama Chetty, *A Manual of Kurnool District in the Presidency of Madras,* (Madras) 1886, pp. 53-55.
41. *Ibid,* p. 53.
42. *Sarojini Regani, Nizam-British Relations: 1724-1857,* Hyderabad, 1963, p. 256.
43. Section, 3 of the Abstract of the Enquiry Commission Report, in *Ibid,* p. 134.
44. Johrapur, located at the confluence of two rivers, Handri and Tunga-bhadra, is today a suburb of the city of Kurnool. N. Gopalakrishnama Chetty, *Ibid,* p. 54.
45. Enquiry Commission Report, Quoted in *The Freedom Struggle, Op.cit.* p. 126.
46. N. Gopalakrishnama Chetty, *A Manual of Kurnool District,* p. 55.
47. *The Freedom Struggle in Hyderabad* (A connected Account), Hyderabad. 1956, 126.
48. See. The taluks of Koilkuntla, Cumbam and Markapur of Cuddapah district and Pattikonda from Bellary District were added to the newly created Kurnool District in 1858 K. Maddaiah, *Freedom Movement in Rayalaseema*, New Delhi, 2012, p. 49.
49. N. Gopalakrishnama Chetty, Ibid. p. 55.
50. *Gazetteer of Nellore District, Brought up to 1938, A Volume*, Madras, 1942, p. 76.
51. Syed Moosa Miah, "The Political Relations Between the Nawabs of Kurnool and the English East India Company : 1702-1839", in the *Proceedings of the Andhra Pradesh History Congress*, IX th. Session, Kurnool, 1985, p. 156.
52. N. Gopalakrishnama Chetty, *Opcit*, p. 55.

# IX

# Mutinies in Military

Opposition to the British rule among the local chiefs like the Zamindars in the Circars and Palegars in the Rayalaseema region was a common feature in the initial decades after the establishment of the Company administration in Andhra, The Revolts of the Vijanagaram Zamindar, the minor Zamindars in the agency area were thus over the heavy peishcush the British collected from them. There were also cases of unrest over the succession issues. The Revolt of Tharnekal( 1801) and the rebellion of Uyyalawada Narasimha Reddy (1846) were due to the denial of pension or compensation amounts due to the Chiefs and headsmen. There was also the fear among such chiefs that their power and authority, they were entitled to over generations, was threatened to be taken away with the arrival of the Company rule. The erosion of such local authority more than anything else drove them to take to arms. The grievances thus were centered on civil affairs concerning land, taxes, local autonomy, exercising authority in their jurisdiction.

Apart from the revolts of the Zamindars and Palegars, there were also Revolts among the ranks of the Company armies in Andhra region at different periods during Pre - 1857 Revolt. While dissatisfaction over service conditions like discrimination in the pay, perks, promotions and leave between European soldiers and

Indian Sepoys are generally cited as potential causes for the *Great Revolt,* the early revolts in the Company's army in Andhra, to a large extent were motivated by religious considerations. These Mutinies by the army men, particularly Muslims, were due to a fear that the Company officials were bent upon destroying their faith and religious practices as they meticulously dismantled their political authority everywhere in the country. Muslims, who got enrolled in large numbers in the Company forces, felt the insecurity whenever the British interfered with their religious practices . As a result, there were instances of Mutinies by Muslim sepoys in the Company army in Andhra and the most important ones were, the Mutiny at Visakhapatnam in 1780, the armed revolt at Mominabad in the Nizam's territory in 1827 and the Bolaram Mutiny, also in Hyderabad in 1855.

## Visakhapatnam Mutiny, 1780

Hailed as the first ever Sepoy Mutiny in India, the Visakhapatnam mutiny took place in 1780, nearly 77 years prior to the Revolt of 1857, regarded as the First war of Independence. It was also much ahead of other Revolts like the Vellore Mutiny (1806)[1] and the mutiny at Gorackpore( (1824). The mutiny at Visakhapatnam was the result of the wrongful decision of the military authorities to send the unwilling troops stationed there to Madras to fight against Hyder Ali of Mysore.[2]

The Visakhapatnam Mutiny was headed by Sheik Mohammad, a Subedar of the Grenadiers Regiment, stationed in Visakhapatnam at that time. During those days, two Regiments of Indian sepoys led by British officers were posted in Visakhapatnam and in Masulipatam. Most of the troopers in both the regiments were Muslims. It was the time when fierce Anglo- Mysore wars were raging in the south and the Company was always in need of extra military to fight Hyder Ali of Mysore.

The Governor of Madras, John Whitehall writing to the Commandant of the Visakhapatnam, James Henry Casmajor, on 14 September, 1780, directed to dispatch a large contingent of his troops to Madras so as to reinforce the Madras regiment to fight against Hyder Ali.

The Sepoys at Visakhapatnam and Masulipatam at that time were a disgruntled lot because the Company refused to pay any remuneration for the tax collection duties they were entrusted with, along with their normal military obligations. Apart from it, they were also averse to the idea of fighting a fellow Muslim, Hyder Ali who by then showed his heroic resistance to the British.

Mutiny broke out when the Visakhapatnam sepoys were asked to board 'Sartine Frigate' the ship, specially sent to bring the troops to Madras. On 3$^{rd}$. October, 1780, at 3 pm, the Commander, Captain. Laysaught, after the inspection of guards, when ordered the troops to board the waiting ship, the sepoys refused to obey his command. Then few other British officers intervened and tried to use force, but the sepoys under the leadership of Shiek Mohammad took up their muskets and fired at the Company officers from close range, killing Lt. Crisps, Cadets Kingsford Venner and Robert Rutherford, the Paymaster. Few other officers were severely injured. Buoyed by the success they had, the rebels at once took hold of the town and captured their Commandant, Casmajor and few more civil servants of the Company. A French national kept as a prisoner by the British on charges of spying, was also set free by the rebels.

The rebels then looted the Company's property and took away all the Rs. 22,000 from the treasury. On the next day, at the intervention of the local Zamindar, Gajapathi Narayan Deo, the Mutineers freed all the captives including J.H. Casmajor, and returned to their posts.

Casmajor then went to the 'Sardine Frigate' and ordered Capt. Ensign Butler to gather the sepoys loyal to the Company and with the help of the crew and the weapons on board, went against the rebels in full vengeance. He also sought the help of the local Zamindar in his swoop against the Mutineers. Many of the rebels were captured and mercilessly killed. Shiek Mohammad, the leader of the rebels also was shot dead.

There is now no reminiscences left of the Visakhapatnam Mutiny of 1780, except for the grave of Capt. Kingsford Venner, in the Old Town Cemetery, with a tombstone intact which states that he was killed in a *'Sepoy Mutiny on 3 Oct. 1780'* . There seems to be no record of graves of other officers killed on that day. Though the Visakhapatnam Mutiny was on a small scale, it did send shock waves for the Company authorities both in India and in England.

## Mutiny At Mominabad: 1827

The Nizam of Hyderabad when came under the British sway by signing the Subsidiary Alliance treaty in October, 1800, he had a vast army that consisted of a contingent of 35,680 infantry, and 34,447 Cavalry, one of the largest of any Indian native prince.[3] While the Infantry was composed of both Hindus and Muslims ,the Nizam's Cavalry was mainly of Muhammadans belonging to different tribes and nationality. They were mostly Patans, Arabs and Daccanies.

After the Nizam entered into the Subsidiary Alliance treaty with the British in October, 1800 AD, several reforms were initiated in the Nizam's forces[4]. Mr. Russell who came as the Resident at Hyderabad in 1811, felt that the army the Nizam was bound to supply as per the subsidiary treaty would not serve any useful purpose unless it was placed on a more efficient footing. So he reformed the entire organization of Nizam's military. He established in 1813 a separate "Russell Brigade" which became a strong instrument of warfare and a model army. It was considered as one of the most disciplined and highly competent battalions in India[5]. In 1815, Russell Brigade played a decisive role to suppress a revolt caused by Mubariz –ud-Daulah, the younger son of Sikandar Jah, the Nizam[6]. Sir Charles Metcalfe who succeeded Russell in 1820 as Resident, made further improvements in the Brigade.

Though the army was called ' Nizam's Contingent' in name, it was for all practical purposes, the Company's Contingent. The Nizam's government that was responsible for the payment of the troops had no administrative control over the contingent. This system gave scope for creating unnecessary posts and paying high salaries for the European military officers. This was well revealed in a popular but sarcastic expression among the Europeans then in India : *"Poor Nizzy! Nizzy pays for all"*.[7]

As the Nizam's troops were trained, armed and clothed on British lines, severe punishments in the name of strict discipline and numerous innovations, hitherto not familiar to the habits and customs of the natives produced a feeling of irritation and resentment among the native soldiers of the Nizam's Contingent. Such a feeling of alienation gave expression in the open defiance, revolt and Mutiny among the Hyderabad's native sepoys on several occasions.

The earliest of such open defiance occurred in 1827 due to an indiscreet act of the British Commandant, at Mominabad in the Hyderabad dominions, who hated the native Sepoys sporting beards and in the name of uniformity, wanted all of them to shave off their beards. On 5 May, one Colonel Davies, to comply with the Commandants orders got two soldiers of the 3rd. Cavalry forcibly got shaved off their beards and also declared that all soldiers "who would not shave their beards voluntarily would be treated in a similar manner".[8] The sepoys were highly peeved over such a step and felt humiliated as keeping beard was a part of their religious custom and prohibiting it was an insult to their religious freedom, they felt.

The next day, the sepoys of the 3rd. Cavalry took position on their parade grounds with loaded guns and decided to defy the Commandant's orders and were ready take vengeance on the Colonel who insulted two of their colleagues on the previous day. When Col. Davies rode up to the infuriated men with confidence to pacify them, he was at once shot by one of them from a close range. When the Colonel fell to the ground, his body was soon cut into pieces by other Mutineers who surrounded him. But soon, all the rebels were at once charged by other soldiers and European officers who were close by. Several of the rioter leaders were instantly shot down while others retreated in haste. A court marshal was established and all those who participated in the mutiny were tried and punished.

The Mutiny of the Nizam's Cavalry at Mominabad revealed that the Indian sepoys were not accustomed to the European discipline. On their part, the European officers were instructed to acquaint themselves with the Indian sentiments and customs. But the severe punishments meted out to the mutineers became a deterrent to the natives to resort to such revolts for a long time thereafter.

## Bolaram Mutiny: 1855

Three decades after the Mominabad revolt, occurred what is familiarly known as *Bolarum Mutiny* that shook the Company administration as never before. Two years earlier to the outbreak of Mutiny at Meerut on 10 May, 1857 that became a prologue for what generally came to be known as the Great Revolt of 1857, there was in Hyderabad a fierce rebellion by a group of cavalry men belonging to the Nizam's contingent stationed at Bolaram in September,1855[9]. The Brigadier- General, Colin Mackenzie, the Commandant of the Regiment, was nearly killed in a daring attack in protest against his blatant orders prohibiting their customary religious procession during Moharam. Colin Mackenzie was so grievously wounded in the attack that he had to leave for England to recoup. The incident attained great significance as his acts which precipitated the revolt were construed even by the administration to be anti-religious. The Bolaram Mutiny became still more significant as the British viewed it later as a forerunner of the large scale country wide outburst of Sepoys against the British during the 1857 Revolt.

## Nizam's Cavalry

Of all the components of the Nizam's army, the cavalry was considered as the finest in the country. It was known for its loyalty and occupied a pride of place even when compared to the infantry. By 1850, the Nizam's Cavalry consisted of nearly ten thousand native Sepoys of all ranks with 84 European officers. It had cantonments spread over several places in the state like Lingsugar, Hindoli, Mominabad, Ellichpur, Aurangabad and Bolaram, each commanded by a seasoned British officer.[10] In 1854, on reorganization of the entire contingent, Brigadier- General, Colin Mackenzie, who earlier had distinguished himself in the Afghan war, was personally picked up by the Governor General Dalhousie and appointed as the Officer Commandant of the Hyderabad Cavalry regiment, stationed in Bolaram.

Brigadier Colin Mackenzie, was a Scottish officer of Indian army who distinguished himself as a Political Agent in Afghanistan. Born in 1806 he joined as a cadet of Madras Native Infantry at the age of 19 and participated in a number of campaigns in South India. In 1840 he was sent to Afghanistan where his services in the First Afghan war and in the capture of Kabul were highly appreciated. Afghans called him as *English Mullah*. Subsequently, he was employed to raise a Sikh Regiment. Mackenzie actively participated in the Second Sikh War (1848) and impressed Lord Dalhousie . In

1850, Dalhousie appointed Mackenzie as the Brigadier General of the Nizam Cavalry in Hyderabad. In selecting Mackenzie for the post, Dalhousie remarked that: "the gallantry, ability and endurance displayed by him at the time of the rising at Kabul are amply recorded..." It was in Hyderabad that Mackenzie faced the Bolaram Mutiny that brought an end to his subsequent military career. Mackenzie had three daughters, the eldest, Rosa Mackenzie was born in Madras in 1835.

It was usual for the Commanding officers of the regiments to grant leave for Muslim troops for ten days at the time of Moharam every year. The festival particularly by the *Shia* sect of Muslims is observed with fast for ten days and on the final big day, a large procession is taken out through the thoroughfares. As in the previous years, the Muslim Cavalry men applied to the Brigadier –General for leave from 14 to 23 September 1855, with the idea that the big Moharam procession would take place on the final day. As 23$^{rd}$. happened to be a Sunday and thus a 'Sabbath Day' for the local Christian officers, Mackenzie felt the Moharam procession will interfere with the social and religious engagements of fellow Christians. He suggested that the observance of Moharam be changed from 23$^{rd}$ to 26$^{th}$. September as the final procession will not be on a Sunday. When Cavalry men were not willing for any such change in their Moharam schedule, Col. Mackenzie altogether prohibited any procession to be held on Sunday, 23 September. His orders, issued on 20$^{th}$ September, said "No procession, music or noise will be allowed on any account whatever, from twelve O' clock midnight on Saturday to twelve O'clock, Sunday night". But on further representation, he modified his orders permitting procession to take place only within the Lines of the Regiments; but not in the barracks or along the roads. The cavalry men felt outrageous as the Commanding officer was humiliating them on religious grounds.

The resentment among the Cavalry men on the ban of the procession became such that they gave vent to their feelings. When the Resident Bushby was returning from a dinner party that evening, the Moharam people near the Cavalry barracks booed at his coach much to his consternation. On the next day, when the two daughters of Colin Mackenzie happened to meet Captain Orr, a deputy of the Brigadier General, he informed them some of the native officers have openly remonstrated against the ban of Moharam procession. But Mackenzie could not assess the anger that was brewing among his men.

On 21st, after sunset, a number of friends and colleagues had come visiting Mackenzie's family. Capt. and Mrs. Orr, the Deputy to the Commandant, Mr. Murry, the Secunderabad Chaplin with his wife; and so was Mrs. And Mr. Carpenter, another deputy of the Brigadier who also joined them. As they all sat with ladies in the open yard in the garden near the gate, a procession making "hideous uproar" of the cavalry men belonging to the 3rd Regiment, was observed by Brigadier General Mackenzie proceeding along the main road in front of his house, the road he had prohibited for the procession.[11]

Mackenzie then asked his Maratha peon, Bapu Rao to tell them to stop the noise though Capt. Orr suggested that they need not be interfered with. But the mob answered that the roads were public and that they would go on procession. At this, the Brigadier, Mackenzie who saw his authority was set at defiance, went out unarmed and reminded the rioters of his orders and asked them to get back to their Lines. As they did not relent, he forcefully seized the two religious *Alums* (sacred standards generally taken in procession during Moharam) they were carrying at the head of the procession. Pulling a sheathed sword from the hands of one of them, Mackenzie struck the man with it in great anger. The orderlies captured, on the orders of the Brigadier, two processionists as 'prisoners', and the rest disappeared. The *Alums* and the sword were retained by the Brigadier. He thought that he has brought the rioters to obedience without knowing that the real trouble was yet to begin.

Soon an armed crowd from the Cavalry Lines furious with rage having been humiliated at the high handed act of the Brigadier-General returned with the war cry, *Din Din.*. The Brigadier and his guests who sat in the garden were alarmed at the shouts of the menacing crowd approaching. The Brigadier Mackenzie hurriedly went out and raised his arm indicating to speak to them. But suddenly a man struck the Brigadier a violent blow with his sword on the head. Several blows followed in quick succession from several sepoys who by then had encircled him. One cut was six inches long another cut took off the middle finger of the right hand. It was found by the doctor who was later summoned from the Residency that there were altogether ten deep cuts all over the body of the Brigadier. Murry, the second in Command who rushed out to save Mackenzie was knocked down. Mrs. Murry received a deep cut, so was Mrs. Carpenter who also was wounded by the mob. Mackenzie seething with pain, and screaming with blood returned with fast paces. But his pursuers did not stop. As he mounted the steps of the house, few gave him "tremendous gashes on the back, one of which was eleven inches long." [12]

Mrs. Mackenzie, who all the time was begging him not to go to the crowd unarmed, got the doors shut after him with the help of the servants while the mutineers kept banging to open. She got all the lamps in the house put off. The severely wounded Brigadier was moved to the old part of the house. Gafoor Khan, Brigadier's standing orderly came from behind and returned to the crowd the two Alums that the Brigadier had seized earlier. He also indicated with signs, to douse the tempers of the mutineers that Mackenzie had "succumbed to the injuries".[13] In the meantime, with the help of Capt. Orr, Mrs. Mackenzie sent for some guards from the infantry division which was stationed near the back of the house. A small body of guards arrived and with that the mob slowly went away. Soon loud noises were heard in the Cavalry lines as they were trumping and loudly laughing in a celebratory mood.

The thickly padded coat that the Brigadier was wearing has actually saved his life. Mrs. Mackenzie washed his wounds and soon sent for the doctor. Dr. Whitelock, the Residency doctor arrived. He soon sewed and dressed up the wounds. The middle finger of the right hand was altogether removed. Capt. Orr went and brought with him a contingent of 3rd infantry to guard Brigadier's house from further attacks. It was also mooted to request the Resident to send for Major General Bell, Commander of the Subsidiary force at Secunderabad. But that day, as the Resident George Alexander Bushby (1853-56) was staying at the house of the Prime Minister, Sir Salar Jung, he could not be disturbed.[14] However, next day, Capt. Orr reported to the Resident that "everything was quiet, and there was no need to send for troops from Secunderabad".

The Resident who also was the Commander-in –Chief of the Nizam's Contingent, was in great fear that there could be general rising among all the Muslims of India which, he felt, "would shake our empire to its foundations". The regiment placed at Mackenzie's house was withdrawn after two days, leaving a small body, on the request by Mrs. Mackenzie, "to guard the Brigadier who was supposed to be dying, should not be again attacked".

On 25th September, the Resident, G.A. Bushby constituted a Court of Enquiry with Major Davidson, the Assistant Resident as Chairman. Major Brice of the Artillery, Major Pritchord, a Judge and Capt. Clogstoun, were the other members. Based on the proceedings of enquiry, which were kept strictly secret, the Governor- General, Lord Dalhousie issued his lengthy final orders.

## Governor General's Orders

Lord Dalhousie, the Governor- General, in- Council, in his General Orders, passed four months after the incident, dated 23rd January, 1856 came heavily on the Brigadier General for "……. he prohibited a Muslim procession on the great Muslim festival, that when the orders were disobeyed, he not only behaved with undue violence but insulted the procession". Mackenzie's act was termed as "Intemperate and unusually stringent and objectionable for it put forward the Moharam in direct conflict with the Christian Sabbath and thus introduced a religious element into the prohibition (of the procession)". On the role of the Brigadier, Dalhousie further stated: "The immediate and real cause of the outrage by which Brigadier Mackenzie has so severely suffered was the act of the Brigadier himself". Dalhousie ordered Mackenzie to proceed on leave to England forthwith to recoup his health.

The Governor General contemplated even to disband the whole Regiment as a punishment, but on second thoughts, decided not to take recourse to so "sweeping a measure."[15]

While several cavalry men and ring leaders, who participated in the attack, were ordered to be dismissed by the Resident, the Governor General himself dismissed from service the native Commissioned officers of the 3rd. Cavalry "as a fitting and effectual measure of punishment". Bhavani Uppidiah and Sumjaun the two Jamedars from infantry guards who came with their men to safeguard Mackenzie's house also were dismissed for not having fired at the mob and defend the Brigadier. "Cowardice in a soldier is as much to be condemned as Mutiny" observed the Governor-General. However, he made few exceptions. Jamedar Shah Mirza Beg who was loyal, was made as Risaldar of the Regiment in the place of Mir Banda Hussain, now dismissed. The loyal orderly of the Brigadier, Gafoor Khan was promoted to the rank of Naib Duffadar.

Dalhousie in the same orders made a general observation exhorting the European officers, "not to interfere with the religious observances of the natives of India under their control, further than what is actually necessary for the preservation of public peace and the maintenance of discipline and order". The Governor General's orders though specifically issued to the Hyderabad contingent in respect of what happened at Bolaram, were communicated to all other Forces and Contingents under the British government in India for their information and guidance.

It is an irony that exactly 15 months after Lord Dalhousie passed those orders on Bolaram case, occurred the Great Revolt in 1857, for the outbreak of which his policies followed as the Governor General were held responsible.[16]

The Bolaram Mutiny had an adverse effect on the subsequent career of Brigadier General Colin Mackenzie. On his return from England, he was appointed for a while as a political representative to the Nawab of Bengal. Then he was transferred to the Civil department of the army as Superintendent of Army clothing, a post obviously inappropriate to the positions held earlier. He was denied every promotion on the ground that he was censured in the Bolaram case.

Mackenzie finally left India in 1873 and died in Edinburgh on 22 October, 1881. Mrs. Helen Mackenzie, the wife of Brigadier Mackenzie, upset with the treatment meted out to her husband by the British government aftermath of Bolaram Mutiny, wrote profusely on the incident in the form of letters and dispatches to " 'Family and friends' in Edinburgh. Her *'Narrative of Mutiny at Bolaram in Sep.1855: For the Information of Brigadier Colin Mackenzie's Family'* is a graphic description of what happened on the day of attack at Bolaram. The narrative, for the obvious Service regulations (Mackenzie was still serving the government in Bengal when she wrote) withheld author's name but only said it was by an anonymous 'Eye Witness Account' . It was printed in Edinburgh by Messrs. Murry and Gib, a private Company. Though it was printed for limited circulation, the narrative which runs into 56 pages ends with a declaration: 'not published'. The booklet, though meant only for Colin Mackenzie's family and "Private friends" found its way to Columbia University Library as late as 2015. Mrs. Helen Mackenzie also published on her husband's turbulent life, *Storms and Sunshine of A Soldier's Life.* The book contains a photograph of Brigadier Mackenzie in Afghan traditional attires with a large turban et al, with the caption, " *Colin Mackenzie, the English Moollah"*[17]

### *New Bungalow for the Commandant*

After the attack on Brigadier Mackenzie, the Nizam, Nasir ud Daulah, decided to build a residence for the Commandant worthy of his power and position with due privacy that will not be vulnerable for any future mob fury.

The Commandant's new residence which took nearly six years for completion, was a single storied attractive bungalow on a sprawling 90 acre site in Bolaram, built with a *Madras type* roof at 20-25 feet height with a low level double pillared common verandah. With about 20 large rooms, it had three wings, a mini theatre and several private halls. The entire bungalow has profuse use of the finest Teak wood. An interesting feature of the building is that an underground 50 meter tunnel connects the kitchen and the dining hall . This was as a precaution to protect the occupant from possible poisoning.

After Hyderabad State was merged with Indian Union, the Commandant's bungalow in Bolaram was taken over by the government of India and was converted into one of the official retreats of the President of India to be used for his winter sojourn, and named it as *Rashtrapati Nilayam*. The other retreat home for the President being *Rashtrapati Nivas* the summer resort, in Shimla. Dr. Rajendra Prasad, the President of India stayed in

Rashtrapati Nilayam in Bolaram during his southern sojourn and the successive Presidents have been using it since then. The government recently has developed landscaped gardens and lawns in Rashrtrapati Nilayam with ornamental shrubs, various species of flowering plants and potted plants.

To the north-west of the building in Bolaram, there was a huge flag-post cum a weather-watch, installed in 1867 but now pulled down. It was here in front of the flag-post that the Prince of Berar, Azam Jah, the second of the Nizam, Osman Ali Khan, as the Hon. Commanding officer of Nizam's forces formally handed over the Hyderabad State to the Indian Union on September 17, 1948, after the "Operation Polo".[18]

## References


1. The Vellore Mutiny, commonly known as 'White Mutiny', occurred when the sepoys apart from resisting the British regulations pertaining to their pay, perks, promotions and other service regulations, also desired to restore Fathe Hyder, the son of Tipu Sultan of Mysore who was incarcerated in Vellore prison along with nearly one hundred family members after the defeat and death of Tipu on 4 May, 1799, for details, see, K. Rajayyan, "The Vellore Mutiny, 1806", in S. Gopalakrishnan, Ed. *The South Indian Rebellions,: Before and After 1800*, Madras, 2007, pp. 33-41.
2. Sumit Bhattacharjee, "Vizag A Poineer in Sepoy Mutiny" *The Hindu, Metro Plus, Visakhapatnam*, Dec. 16, 2002.
3. Political Consultations, 24 February, 1797, No.7, Quoted in Nani Gopal Chaudhuri, *British Relations With Hyderabad,(1798- 1843)*, University of Calcutta, 1964, p. 195.
4. For a detailed analysis of the terms of the Subsidiary treaty entered between the Nizam Ali Khan and the British, see, Henry George Briggs, *The Nizam: His History and Relations with the British Government,* Vol I, 1861, rpt. Delhi, 1985, p. 80.
5. Raza Alikhan, *Hyderabad, 400 Years (1591-1991)* Hyderabad, 1991, p. 206.
6. K.S.S. Seshan, "Of Passion, Rebellion and Conspiracy", *The Hindu, Metro Plus,* Hyderabad, 10 June, 2017, p. 4 The Nizam's Contingent also played a key role during the 1857 Revolt by helping Sir Hugh Rose in his fight

against Jhansi. In 1903,Hyderabad Cavalry was merged with the Indian army and was renamed as *Deccan Horse. Deccan Horse* played a significant role in France and Palestine during World War I and was honored with the prefix, "Royal". However, on India becoming a Republic in 1950, 'Royal' was dropped. Today, Deccan Horse is a renowned Tank Regiment of the Indian Army. For details, Raza Alikhan, Ibid, p. 207.

7. Nani Goal Chaudhuri, *British Relations with Hyderabad,( 1798-1843),* University of Calcutta, 1964, Op.cit. p. 195.
8. Burton, History of Hyderabad Contingent, p. 109, quoted in Nani Gopal Chaudhuri *Ibid,*, p. 196.
9. K.S.S. Seshan, "Protest Over a Procession", *The Hindu, Metro Plus,* Hyderabad, October, 2, 2017, p. 5.
10. Raza Alikhan, Hyderabad 400, *Op.cit,* pp. 193-207.
11. *"Narrative of the Mutiny at Bolarum in September,1855: For Information of Brigadier Colin Mackenzie's Family and Private Friends".* Edinburgh, 1857, Here after, Narrative of the Mutiny at Bolarum......
12. *Narrative of the Mutiny at Bolaram,* Ibid.
13. This was obviously to instill fear and evoke empathy among the mutineers. It must be on the suggestion made by Mrs. Helen Mackenzie, the wife of the Brigadier.
14. G.A. Bushby was the first of the British Residents to die in Hyderabad. He died on 30 December, 1856 after being in office for three years. Incidentally, Cuthbert Davidson, his successor as regular Resident also died in Hyderabad in August, 1862. Arthur Austin Roberts in 1868 and Stuart Mitford Fraser in 1916 were the other serving Residents to die in Hyderabad. For details, see, Reza Ali Khan, *Hyderabad 400 Years (1591-1991)* Hyderabad, 1991, pp. 134-135.
15. *Narrative of the Mutiny at Bolaram,* Ibid.
16. The Governor General, Dalhousie's policies, particularly the sequestering of Indian native states in the name of maladministration, the passing of the "Doctrine of Lapse" disregarding the Hindu law of primogeniture, and the introduction of Railways for the twin purposes of exporting Indian agricultural raw materials and for transporting the imported British *machinofactures* from the port cities to the hinterland markets were largely cited as responsible factors for the 1857 Revolt. Being conscious of his responsibility for the entire tragedy that was 1857 Revolt, Dalhousie proscribed the publication of all his private papers for fifty years after his demise.
17. *K.S.S. Seshan, Protest over a Procession, op.cit,* p. 5.

18. Prince Azam Jah, known familiarly as "The Prince of Berar", was the elder of the two sons of Mir Osman Ali Khan, the Nizam VII. He served as the Hon. Commandant of the Nizam's forces before the State was integrated with Indian Union in September, 1948.

## Chapter - X

# Narasimha Reddy Revolt: (1846)

Of all the anti- British rebellions in Andhra during the pre-1857 phase, the most violent and most severe one was the revolt of Uyyalawada Narasimha Reddy in 1846. The revolt put the entire Ceded District into a ferment. The revolt of Narasimha Reddy of Uyyalawada[1] (in Koilkuntla Taluk of present day Kurnool District) attained significance as a large number of dispossessed Kattubadidars participated in it. The most important reason for Narasimha Reddy to rebel against the British was the refusal of the government to accede his request to extend him the pension of his maternal grand mother, a daughter of the Nossum Palegar.

The Palegar of Nossum, in the then Cuddapah District (it was transferred to Kurnool District in 1858.) was one of the eighty Palegars put down by Thomas Munro, the first Principal Collector. Like many other Palegars, the Palegar of Nossum also refused to attend the cutcheri (camp office) of the Collector, declined to clear the arrears of his rent and when pressure was mounted, absconded after some resistance. Munro took to his usual recourse of sending the military which captured the Palegar. The Palegar of Nossum was imprisoned in the fort of Gooty by Munro.

About the Nossum chiefs Munro has graphically recounted in his Memorandum on the Poligars of the Ceded Districts, that he prepared and submitted to the Government of Madras, after being appointed as the Principal Collector. According to it, the ancestors of the Nossum family served the Vijayanagar rulers as the Patels (Village heads) and also as Deshmukhs of Combum, having an army of around two thousand. In those days they had about 54 villages under their control, valued at 10 thousand pagodas. After the fall of Vijayanagar, when Golconda Sultans held this region, few villages were resumed from the Palegar and he was levied an amount of 7,800 Pagodas per year.

In 1776 Hyder Ali of Mysore took possession of the Palem when he conquered this area but after the defeat of Tipu Sultan, in the Third Mysore war in 1792, the Nizam of Hyderabad got this area as his share. One, Jayarami Reddy was the Palegar on whom Nossum was settled by the Nizam's administration for an annual payment of Rs. 80,000. But as the amount was heavy, the Palegar paid not more than 45,000 a year. In 1794, under the threat of military action by the Nizam, the Palegar agreed to pay the following amounts:

| | | |
|---|---|---|
| Net Peishcush of Nossum | | Rs. 45,000 |
| Nizam's increase | | Rs. 37,500 |
| | | Rs. 82,500 |
| Durbar Nuzzar | + | Rs. 5,625 |
| | | Rs. 88,125 |
| The Palegar Paid only | – | Rs. 37,000 |
| The balance left | | Rs. 51,125[2] |

Chandulal, the Prime minister of the Nizam had no hope of collecting such a huge balance due from the Palegar. When Thomas Munro took charge as the Principal Collector, in November, 1800, the Nizam's armies were busy with the seize of Nossum. On Munro's intervention through his Amildar, the Nizam's army was at once withdrawn.

Munro fixed a reduced rent of Rs. 45,000 on the Nossum Palegar and directed him to pay in three installments. But as the Palegar did not pay even the first installment, Munro decided to resume the Nossum Palem and pension off the Palegar. About this, Munro had stated thus:

> "But as he (the Palegar of Nossum) did not pay the first till after the last had become due, and as there was not the smallest possibility of his paying the rest, it became necessary to deprive him of the management of the District (Palem) as the only way of securing a future revenue"[3]

An army under General Campbell was dispatched against Nossum, which after a surprise attack, imprisoned the Palegar. The Palem was resumed by the government and a pension was settled on the dispossessed Palegar. The pension thus granted was Rs. 8,323 being 10% of the revenues of the Palem. After the death of the Palegar, the pension was continued to his widow as the Palegar was childless.[4] A portion of it was continued to the two sisters of the dead Palegar, who were married to the neighboring Palegar of Uyyalawada. It was this portion of the pension that Uyyalawada Narasimha Reddy claimed after their death, through a petition and on the refusal of which he decided to revolt against the British.

## Uyyalawada's Claims

The Palegar of Uyyalawada was granted a monthly pension of Rs 70 after it was sequestrated by Munro during 1800-1801, as the Palem was much smaller in its extent. But the main financial support for this family came from the widow of the Nossum Palegar. But on her death, the Pension was stopped (as she had no children). A portion of the pension that was extended to the two sisters of the Nossum chief, who were married into Uyyalawada family, also stopped after their demise. Therefore, Uyyalawada family was left only with a meager amount of Rs 70 that was due to them. After some years, this pension was divided among the two sons of the Palegar and each one got Rs 35 a month. One of these brothers, as mentioned earlier, had married the two sisters of the Nossum Palegar and had three sons. These sons being the descendants of the last Palegar of Nossum from the mother's side, put forth their claims for the pension that was granted to their maternal grandfather. Their claim was rejected and they had for their support only Rs. 35, being their father's share of the original pension.[5]

While Narasimha Reddy was a grandson of the Uyyalawada Palegar in the male line, he was also a grandson on his mother's side to the Nossum Chief. Being one of the three brothers, he got Rs.11-10-8 (one third of Rs.35). But if he were to be treated from the Nossum line, he would get a more handsome amount of pension. Therefore he decided to fight claiming a share in the Nossum pension. However, his two other brothers, Kumara Malla Reddy and Varada Reddy reconciled to what has been their share of the Uyyalawada pension and did not cooperate with Narasimha Reddy in his revolt. [6]

Narasimha Reddy in his fight against the British, had the support of several chiefs of the day. The Rajas of Wanaparthi, Munagala, Jataprolu, Owk and Penugonda were rumored to be sympathetic to the revolt of Reddy. There were also several prominent leaders among his followers like Gosayi Venkanna, Dasari Roshi Reddy, Jangam Malliah, Karanam Aswathama and others. Several Kattubadidars who were dispossessed of their Inam lands and also lower peasantry and the tribals like the Odderas, the Chenchus and Yanadies also joined the ranks of Narasimha Reddy.[7] Gosayi Venkanna of Akumalla village was a confident and a family priest of Narasimha Reddy. He is said to have instigated him to take to arms and recover what was rightfully due to him from the government. He seems to have also predicted that he would be successful in his fight against the government. He had assured Narasimha Reddy that the "British bullets cannot pierce through his body as he was invincible". Reddy had great faith in whatever Venkanna predicted.

Narasimha Reddy's plan was to initiate a rebellion and then withdraw to some hill fortress with his followers and hold on until he could make the government to come to terms and grant him his demands. This was also evidenced by the fact that among the papers discovered in his possession later, there was a draft of a letter that he addressed to the Board of Revenue expressing his desire to pay allegiance to the Company administration if his demands were met.[8]

In June 1846, followed by about 30 trusted men, Narasimha Reddy went round the villages in both Uyyalawada and Nossum Palems where he was popular and persuaded the Kattubadi Inamdars whose Inam lands it was feared that the Company was planning to resume. There was great enthusiasm among the Kattubadidars who started to swell in their ranks in support of Reddy. Having come to know of the movements of Narasimha Reddy, the Thahasildar of Koilkuntla, in whose jurisdiction was his Palem, sent his men to fetch him. But Narasimha Reddy not only did not comply, but on contrary, even harassed the officials who came to meet him with the summons. The party of the Thahasildar with a body of peons and a contingent of nearly 100 Kattubadies was attacked by Narasimha Reddy with his troops. He captured all the peons and imprisoned them in his fort while the Kattubadidars deserted the Company service and joined the rebel leader.[9] This was a clear indication that the Kattubdidars supported Reddy from the very beginning.

## Attack on the Treasury

Enthused by the success, Narasimha Reddy collected more number of followers. Soon the number rose to 300 and with such a body of Kattubadidars, he led an attack on the Thahasildar's office in Koilkuntla and looted the treasury. A Duffedar and few guards at the treasury tried to defend the treasury building. They fired at the rebels from the roof top, killing few and wounding many. But Narasimha Reddy took out a matchlock and aimed at the Duffedar killing him instantaneously.[10] He then marched away with the booty along with his army to the Kurnool borders. Kurnool, at that time was a non-regulatory region.[11] By then, Narasimha Reddy's army swelled to nearly five thousand strong.

Narasimha Reddy attended the annual fair at Rudravaram. When the Thahasildar came to know of it, he along with his sibbandi made a futile attempt to capture the Palegar. Narasimha Reddy plundered the village, Rudravaram and in the process, killed the Head Duffedar and his nine peons, employed by the government. He also killed Peter, the forest Ranger and few of his forest officials, who were said to be corrupt and behaved towards people in tyrannical manner.

At the time of Narasimha Reddy's attack on the treasury, the Collector, Cochrane was at Madanapalle where there was the summer residence for the Cuddapah Collector.[12] He at once sent instructions to the military stationed at Cuddapah and hastened to the headquarters. The Collector in his letter of 20 July, 1846, asked the government of Madras to announce a reward of Rs. 10,000, for the arrest of Narasimha Reddy. By then, Narasimha Reddy's forces kept on increasing. He crossed the Nallamala forests and marched to attack Cumbam, the seat of a Sub-Collector. On the way at Giddalur, he was met by Col. Watson who marched with a force of 100 men followed by the Thahasildar and few peons. Col. Watson finding himself opposed by a large army of more than five thousand of the rebel forces, withdrew himself into a ruined fort where he took shelter for about six hours. He then attacked the Palegar and killed nearly 200 of his men. However in this conflict, the Thahasildar of Cumbam was killed . He was shot through the head by one of the men of the Palegar, when standing on the walls of the old fort. Then Narasimha Reddy withdrew to Mundlapadu and Watson himself retreated to

Satyavole, about five miles from Cumbam, with his troops[13]. Narasimha Reddy then proceeded to Krishnamsettipalle in Cumbam taluk and plundered it.

In the meantime, another force of about 250 men under Capt. Nott of the 19th. Native infantry was pressed into service. It arrived on 24 June, 1846 and camped within five miles where Narasimha Reddy was believed to have retreated. Capt. Nott was joined by another contingent under Capt. Russell, the Assistant Commissioner of Kurnool. The combined troops started chasing the rebels. Few sepoys of Capt. Nott were killed at Giddalur and also at Mundlapadu. But the English had a major reverse when Capt. Russell was shot dead by Narasimha Reddy. But Capt. Nott was able to kill about 25 and capture many more of the rebels. With this sudden setback, many of the followers of Reddy fled from the scene. Then the Palegar plundered several places like Owk, Nossum and Munnemgudu and decamped with arms and provisions for his men. He then proceeded towards Kothakota, where his family had been left. After this reversal, the Palegar himself took shelter in the thick Nallamala forests.[14]

It was believed that Narasimha Reddy fled to Hyderabad territory and therefore a regiment of troops was summoned on the request of the Collector of Cuddapah, from Secunderabad to the borders in order to apprehend him in case he crossed the river, Krishna. But as there was no sign of Narasimha Reddy entering the Nizam territory, the army regiment was duly sent back to the barracks.

After about six weeks, Narasimha Reddy reappeared on the hills close to Uyyalawada. He had about 400 followers with him. It was thought that he was planning to attack the town, Cuddapah. Four companies of armies were at once sent into the field. Narasimha Reddy with his men proceeded and took position in a pagoda on Perusomala hill.[15]

## Capture of the Palegar

The armies of Kurnool stationed at Perusomala sent several Sawaras to the nearest posts. Soon the hill was surrounded by the Sawaras and information was sent to the Collector, Cochrane. He immediately arrived with Capt. Nott, Capt. Younghusband and Lieutenant Newlyn of the 19$^{th}$. Regiment. They were directed by Colonel Grantham to proceed to the posts assigned to them. The Collector's assistants, Thornhill and Smith rode in advance to ensure the proper spread of the Sawaras around the hill. The British troops thus encircled the Perusomala hill and the Palegar was almost immobilized. After some resistance, Narasimha Reddy was captured and 40 to 50 of his men were killed in the encounter while around 90 were captured as prisoners. Narasimha Reddy was slightly injured in the leg, but not seriously. Reddy's close followers like Roshi Reddy, Gosayi Venkanna and others were also captured at various places. Some others were apprehended in the Muktal division in the Hyderabad state.

## Public Hanging of Narasimha Reddy

The Court Martial (Fouzdaree Adalat) which tried the case of Narasimha Reddy, after taking all the circumstances into consideration, came to the opinion that the proof against the prisoner, Narasimha Reddy was sufficient enough to commit him to the crime of "Rebellion, murder and robbery". He was charged under the provisions of Section 2 of Regulation I of 1834 and section 10 of Regulation VIII of 1802. The Court Martial sentenced him to death penalty, and prescribed that "after being hanged, his body was to be suspended in chains in a cage on a high gibbet to be erected on the spot".

On 22 February, 1847, Narasimha Reddy was paraded in chains in the streets of Koilkuntla and was hanged at 7 A.M. on the banks the river, Jurreru, in the presence of a large gathering of the villagers. His skeleton in chains was kept in a cage in the outskirts of Koilkuntla. As a latter Collector testified in his writing about it in 1875, "Narasimha Reddy was hanged at Koilkuntla and his body exposed in chains where the bones still continue to this day as a warning to bad characters"[16] His severed head was kept on the fort wall of Koilkuntla as a ghastly reminder of the valiant rebellion of Narasimha Reddy.

## Inquiry Commission

One of the immediate results of the revolt of Narasimha Reddy was the appointment of a one- man Commission under Mr. Inglis, by the government of Madras to deal with all the aspects of the revolt in a comprehensive way. It was also to try all those captured during the course of the revolt. It is to be noted that in his report, Inglis attributed the rising to a general feeling of discontent among the Kattubadidars in the District, which had been prevalent for quite some years. There was also a fear among them that they would lose their Inam lands due to the introduction of new Police organization. Inglis was right as at that time, the government was contemplating such a reorganization of the Police set up in the Presidency.

The report of Inglis turned out to be so significant that the government decided to adopt a more liberal policy towards the Inam tenures in the light of the revolt of Narasimha Reddy. For a careful investigation into the validity of Inam holdings, a separate Commission was appointed with G.N. Taylor as the Inam Commissioner. The Inam Commission Report gave definite guidelines in matters of the Inam lands and thus the indiscriminate resumptions by the government stopped. [17]

Though the government felt that the revolt of Narasimha Reddy politically was of no great consequence, on the economic side, it thoroughly altered British attitude towards Inam tenures in South India.[18] The establishment of the Inam Commission was thus the direct result of the revolt of Narasimha Reddy.

Cochrane, the Collector of Cuddapah, in his report on the role of the Kattubadidars in the revolt, dated 15 April, 1847, stated that the disaffection was not a major phenomenon and it was only a local one. "The cause was not so much about the discontent of the Kattubadies as that of the ambition of the leader, Narasimha Reddy"[19].

In the aftermath of the revolt, the Collector, Cochrane was found fault by the government for "acting with too much of self confidence and quickly withdrawing the troops and thereby giving scope to the rebel leader to gain time and muster support in the process"[20].

However, several studies made on the nature and content of Narasimha Reddy's revolt in recent decades, have established that it was also a 'peasant' revolt as many peasants, artisans and Kattubadi Inamdars who were denied of their '*service* Inam lands' (generally rent free lands) participated in it because of the government's policy of indiscriminate sequestrating the Inams[21].

Though more than one hundred and sixty years passed since the revolt of Narasimha Reddy, his heroic exploits against the British are still fresh in the minds of the people in the Rayalaseema region. Recently, a memorial committee to commemorate Narasimha Reddy's Revolt has been formed with a view to raise a fitting monument to the Palegar at Jagannathakonda near Koilkuntla. The committee consisting of several prominent politicians and local leaders of Kurnool District, has plans to erect a statue of Narasimha Reddy and publish literature pertaining to his revolt.[22]

The revolt of Narasimha Reddy had obviously shaken the Company administration and the numerous Commissions which later came into being amply testifies it. The story of the revolt of Narasimha Reddy has remained in the minds and hearts of the people of Rayalaseema till today. There are a number of Ballads and Folk songs on the heroism and reckless valour of Narasimha Reddy and the exemplary courage he exhibited while fighting against the British.[23] His daring attack on the treasury at Koilkuntla and the murder of the Company officials are highly spoken by the people of this region even now. The revolt though was not successful, has become a source of inspiration to the future generations in despising the British rule. Narasimha Reddy's revolt was certainly one of the significant revolts in the country during the pre-1857 phase.

## References

1. Uyyalawada in Koilkuntla Taluk is located on the banks of Kundu, a tributary to river Penna. Kundu, because of its frequent floods that bring heavy damage to Nandyala region, is popularly known as 'Sorrow of Nandyala'. In ancient times, Kundu was known as Kumudwathi. There is a belief locally that whoever drinks the water in Kundu will gain enormous courage to face any enemy. The Kundu valley is known for *pourusham,* i.e. valour.
2. N. Gopalakrishnama Chetty, A Manual of Kurnool District in the Presidency of Madras, Reprint, Hyderabad, 1992, p. 88.
3. Thomas Munro's *Memorandum on the Palegars of the Ceded Districts*, Section, 22 on Koilkuntla.
4. J.D.B. Gribble, *Manual of Cuddapah District,* Madras, 1875, p. 122.
5. J. Hanumatsasthri, "Uyyalawada Narasimha Reddy", Tel. *Andhra Pradesh,* Telugu Monthly, (Director, Information and Public Relations, Hyderabad,, December, 1974, pp. 40-42.
6. Official Report of J.H. Cochrane, Acting Collector and Magistrate, Cuddapah, Dt. 15 April, 1847 to the Secretary, to government, Judicial Department. In Cuddapah District Records, A.P. State Archives Hyderabad.
7. H. Heera Lal, "Kurnool Zillah Samagra Swatantra Rajakeeya Charithra,", *Andhra Pathrika*, March, 19, 1897, p. I-IV.
8. J.D.B. Gribble, *op.cit,* p. 143.
9. J.D.B. Gribble, op.cit.
10. According to oral testimony, the head of the Duffedar was severed, placed in an earthen pot and carried off by the rebel leader in an act of vengeance against the government.

11. After the revolt of Nawab Gulam Rasool Khan in 1839, Kurnool was kept as non-regulation region under a Commissioner. At the time of Narasimha Reddy's revolt, the Commissioner of Kurnool was H.D. Phillip. See for details, N.Gopalakrishnama Chetty, *op.cit*. p. 56.
12. It may be recalled that Mr. Lacon, the Collector was away in Madanapalle when the Assistant Sub-Collector, Macdonald was murdered in 1832. The details of Macdonald's murder are discussed in an earlier Chapter.
13. J.D.B. Gribble, *op.cit*, p. 114.
14. Official Report of J.H. Cochrane, the Acting Collector and Magistrate, Cuddapah, to Secretary to Government, Judicial Department, Ft. St. George, Madras. dated, 15 April, 1847.
15. J.D.B. Gribble, *op.cit*, p. 115.
16. J.D.B. Gribble, op.cit, p. 115.
17. The Inam Commission was appointed on 16 November, 1858 with G.N. Taylor as the first Commissioner, For details of the circumstances under which the Inam Commission was established, see, the Minutes of W.T. Blair, to R.A. Dalyel, Secretary to government, no. 55, 30 October, 1869.
18. This view is also expressed by few scholars. For details, see, Dharma Kumar, *Land and Caste in South India, Agricultural Labour in the Madras Presidency, During the Nineteenth Century,* Cambridge, 1965.
19. Official Report of J.H. Cochrane, Acting Collector and Magistrate, Cuddapah, Dated, 15 April, 1847,to the Secretary, to Government, Judicial Department, Fort St. George, Madras.
20. J.D.B. Gribble, op.cit. p. 116.
21. Y.V. Krishna Rao, *Andhra Pradesh Lo Swathantranikimundu Rythu Poratalu Rythu Sanghalu,* Vijayawada, 1981, p. 7.
22. The Memorial Committee consists among others, Silpa Chakrapani Reddy,( President), Kaipa Prathapa Reddy, Kasipuram Prabhakar Reddy, Gangula Jagannatha Reddy and others as members., See *Saakshi,* Telugu, Kurnool District Tabloid.
23. There are particularly in the Kurnool region, several folk songs eulogizing his heroism. The Ballad on Narasimha Reddy is sung as popular Burrakatha. See, Dharani Ramachandra Rao, op.cit, p. 76. It is also reported in the press that a feature film in Telugu is being planned with Mr. Chiranjeevi, a popular film hero in the lead. It is said that it will be his 151st. film, in case it happens.

# XI

# Conclusions

The 1857 Rebellion was preceded by a wave of sporadic revolts in the late $18^{th}$. and the first half of the $19^{th}$ centuries. The thrust of these revolts was to contest the nature of changes that were brought by the British East India Company. The Company's administrators tried to reorder an existing feudal setup in the first century of its rule in order to ensure the political and economic stability of the empire. This process led to severe discontent among the traditional landlords, Zamindars and Palegars. Even the peasant classes comprising of cultivators, rural armed constabulary as well as the landless labourers who depended on agriculture and its allied sectors for survival were the participating elements in such revolts.

There were few distinct processes that led to the revolts between 1757 and 1857. The most important one was the land revenue settlement that structured all the British policies. The land tenures were also accompanied by basic reforms in matters of collection of land revenue where the fixation of the revenue was done by the Company officials and not the traditional Zamindars or the Palegars. The British promulgated rules in which the lands of the defaulters could be auctioned to a new class of land holders. This meant that the traditional land holders who hitherto had the power and authority on the peasants were to lose their hold. This created a class of disgruntled Palegars and Zamindars who provided leadership to many revolts of the period either themselves or through their military.

The pre- 1857 revolts were wide spread and they occurred almost in every part of the country. Opposition to British rule in India began almost from the very beginning of the establishment of their rule. The nature of the British rule was such that it invited revolts and rebellions. As the Company administration tried to alter the existing feudal order, there was severe discontent among the Zamindars, Palegars and other traditional land holders. The numerous land revenue systems introduced by the British with a view to maximize their income, distanced every section of people involved with land.

Land under the Company administration was transformed in to a state property. Land tax, particularly in Madras, was always high. The government collected in cash and to the last pie. Failure to pay the rents on time, led to the sequestration of the estates or the Zamindari. Though the tribals, planters and artisans and weavers were also affected by the colonial policies and showed their resentment, the Palegars and Zamindars as they had military under their control, often resorted to revolts.

There were a number of armed rebellions all over the country during the century from 1757 to 1857. The Santhal and Sanyasi rebellions, the Mopilla revolts in the Malabar, the Chakma disturbances, the Kol and the Khasi disturbances, the Khond rebellions etc. were all indicative of the anti-colonial tendencies. In South India there were major revolts by leaders like the Veera Pandya Kattabomman, Yusuf Khan, the Maruthu brothers and several others in the Madurai region. The revolts of Veluthambi of Travancore, Pazhassi Raja in the Malabar and Rani Chennamma of Kittur in Karnataka were significant. In Andhra the revolts were brought out by Zamindars in the Northern Circars and by the Palegars in the Rayalaseema as well as in Chittoor.

The Seemandhra region was acquired by the British in three stages. In 1766 the Northern Circars were got from Nizam Ali while Rayalaseema, comprising of the Districts of Cuddapah, Kurnool, Bellary and Anantapur, was ceded to the Company in 1800 after the Subsidiary alliance of Lord Wellesley was signed by the Nizam. Thomas Munro who was appointed as the first Principal Collector for the Ceded Districts, became famous as the author of the Ryotwar settlement after he conducted experiments in the land revenue administration in the Ceded districts. In 1801, when the Arcot Nawabi was dispossessed, Chittoor and Nellore Districts were brought under the control of the British. Thus the entire Seemandhra came under the control of the Company administration by diplomatic maneuvers and not by any war.

Almost immediately after the occupation of the territories, the British faced revolts from the Zamindars in the Northern Circars and by the Palegars in the Ceded Districts as well as in the Chittoor District. Most of the revolts were due to the changes in the land revenue policies. The revolts were caused by the steps taken by the Company government from time to time to collect the rents strictly and to prevent accumulation of heavy arrears. There were also internal disturbances specially among the Hill chiefs, who quarreled among themselves making the government's interference inevitable.

After the acquisition of the Northern Circars, there were a number of rebellions against the British by the Zamindars in the Ganjam area. The higher rates of land rents was the primary reason for such revolts. As the Company administration was in great need of money for its profits as well as for conducting various military campaigns, the assessment on lands was always high. The Zamindars in the Ganjam District resented to such high rates of rents and resorted to rebellions. There was also the constant fear among them that their Zamindaries would be sequestrated if they failed to discharge the dues on time. The Company administration felt that the Zamindars would be more amenable to law if they had no armies under their control and therefore disbanded such armies. The Company officials acted ruthlessly against the Zamindars, the weavers and other artisans.

The Zamindars in Ganjam, like Parlakimidi, Gumsur, Vijayanagar etc. gave constant trouble to the Company by refusing to pay the tribute. These Zamindars, accustomed to traditional authority over their subjects and who enjoyed almost independent existence from the suzerain authorities, found the Company administration denying such an autonomy. The new regulations the British introduced in matters of collection of rents meticulously was looked as undermining their power and authority. The Zamindars who earlier entertained a feeling that they had a right over the life and death of their subjects, now were made answerable to the government even for the slightest of punishments they inflicted on their subjects. The loss of traditional authority was something the Zamindars could not reconcile to. Rebellion therefore became a natural corollary.

The hilly terrain in the Ganjam Zamindaries was conducive for the gorilla tactics which they commonly adopted whenever the British troops were sent to suppress them. Zamindars like Narayana Deo of Parlakimidi and Sikhara Bhanj of Gumsur gave protracted trouble to the British armies with their rebellions. The Company administration created uncertainty among the Chiefs by making and unmaking of the Zamindars. Many of these dispossessed Zamindars were sent away as prisoners to Vellore.

Several tribals like Savaras, Khonds, Bhills etc. added to the disorders by raiding the villages and plundering. In Ganjam there were a number of Sowcars who lent money to the Zamindars at exorbitant rates of interest and caused havoc in the socio-economic scenario.

It was Vizianagaram Zamindar who faced the British in a decisive battle in 1794. Though Viziarama Raju lost the battle of Padmanabham, his opposition to the British became an epitome of inspiration to many other chiefs in Andhra. Vizianagaram, the most prominent of all the Andhra Zamindaries, played a very significant role in the politics of the day both under the French as well as under the Company administration. General Bussy took the help of Vizianagaram in the Bobbili war (1757) using the traditional rivalry between Vizianagaram and Bobbili. During the period of Viziarama Raju II (1760-94) the Zamindari played an important role in the fortunes of the British in the Circars. Though he was beset with internal bickering due to his Diwan Sitharama Raju, the Zamindar was able to consolidate his power and played a decisive role in his relations with the Company. He was instrumental in inviting Col. Forde with an army to oust the French influence in the Northern Circars.

Notwithstanding the help extended by Viziarama Raju, the British started treating him in a ruthless manner. The way the much hated Diwan, Sitharama Raju was re-appointed against the will of the Zamindar and imposing very harsh conditions after the Circuit Committee report were resented even by the Court of Directors. When it was decided to divest him of his Zamindari with a paltry pension, Viziarama Raju decided to oppose the British.

The Padmanabham battle (1794) in which Viziarama Raju was defeated and killed was a watershed in the annals of the history of Andhra. Though the Zamindari was restored to Narayan Gajapathi Raju, the son of the deceased Zamindar, the territory was much reduced and his powers truncated. All the dependent minor Zamindaries were also taken out of the Vizianagaram control. In 1802, when the Permanent Settlement was implemented, Vizianagaram Zamindari was settled as per the new regulations.

The example of Vizianagaram Zamindar was taken by several small and Hill Zamindars in opposing the British. The Zamindars like Kasipuram, Palakonda, Golugonda, Mogulturru etc. revolted due to the steps taken by the government from time to time in collecting the rents and to prevent accumulation of heavy arrears. In most cases the government dispossessed the rebellious Zamindars and sequestrated their estates. In some cases, the rebellious Zamindars were removed and were replaced by their kin, as in the case of Palaconda Zamindari when Vijayarama Raj was deposed and his son, Sitharama Raj was made as the Zamindar. There were also few rebellions on the amounts payable as pensions after the removal of the Zamindars. The Zamindar of Kasipuram rose in revolt in 1830 due to the denial of the pension. In the case of the Hill Zamindars also, George Russell and his armies played a key role in the suppression of their rebellions.

In the Ceded Districts and in Chittoor, Company administration had to face the numerous revolts of the Palegars. When Thomas Munro took over at the Principal Collector of the Ceded districts in November, 1800, he had under him four subordinate Collectors stationed at Cuddapah, Cumbam and at Adoni. In the entire Ceded Districts there were 80 Palegars and their army men exceeded thirty thousand.

Munro who earlier worked under Col. Reid had definite ideas about the "Ryotwari" system of land revenue which he was bent upon introducing in the Ceded Districts. The suppression of the Palegars therefore became inevitable. Munro was permitted by the government to correspond directly without routing his correspondence through the Board of Revenue. As he had a limited number of army men at his disposal, Munro decided to deal with the Palegars with caution. The methods adopted by the Palegars and the reaction from Munro were almost the same in every case. On the failure of the Palegars in discharging their rents, the Collector sends the army to capture such Palegars. The Palem is sequestrated and armies disbanded. The occupied lands are then brought under the Ryotwari. This was the usual way followed by Munro in dealing with the Palegars.

It should be remembered that Thomas Munro though acted harshly against the rebellious Palegars, he was very humane in treating the peasants from whom he tried to collect the rents directly and to whom he assigned lands and issued the title deeds (Pattas). He earned the goodwill of the peasants though incurred the wrath of the Palegars.

The Palegars in the Ceded Districts unlike their counterparts in Chittoor, failed to give a united front to the Government. They all acted independently and therefore were easily put down. With the systematic survey and settlement, the elaborate administrative machinery and above all by being always on the move in the midst of the people, Thomas Munro successfully won the hearts of the common people of the Ceded Districts making Palegars as outdated and redundant. The good work done in this regard by Munro was duly acknowledged by even the Company Directors at home.

The murder of Macdonald, the young Additional Sub-Collector in Cuddapah in 1832 was a major event in the District which the Company officials termed it only as the work of a frenzied mob. But in reality it turned out to be the work of the Wahabis who wanted to foment anti-British sentiment among the people in Cuddapah.

At the time the British took control of the Ceded Districts, there were scarcities and famines, but the Company administration went ahead with the collection of land taxes unmindful of the economic grievances of the farmers. It is no wonder that the dissatisfied peasants were ready to support any revolt against the colonial administration. The Tharnekal Revolt in 1801 was the first major rebellion against the British in the Ceded Districts in the wake of the Company's acquisition of the Ceded Districts. The enhancement of the land revenue by the new administration was the chief cause for the revolt. The administration also tried to make use of the traditional rivalry between the two villages, by setting one against the other. The Sheristhadar, Srinivasa Rao, with a view to intimidate Gowdappa and the ryots of Thornekal, made use of the leaders of Pasaladinne as informers to ascertain the assessment amounts collected from the village during the former regime.

When the villagers under Muthukur Gowdappa decided to defy the British army, it is clear that they never estimated the strength of the Company forces under William Thackeray, nor they imagined the kind of arms and ammunition they possessed. The conventional weapons the villagers used were no match for the superior arms the British possessed. Though the resistance failed, the inspiration it provided is still to be discerned as a kind of legacy among the youth of this region.

The revolt of the Chittoor Palegars in 1804 was in many respects different from that of the rebellions of the Palegars in the Ceded Districts. The Chittoor Palegars acted with a unity of purpose. They became hostile to the British because their suzerain, the Nawab of Arcot was unceremoniously removed from power. They were also displeased at the loss of their traditional power over their subjects. When the first two Collectors, Stratton and Cockburn tried to introduce a system of land revenue that was completely different to the existing conventional one, the Palegars only felt aggrieved.

The Chittoor Palegars had their fortifications and when their Kattubadi armies were removed, they decided to fight the Company forces to safeguard their traditional power and authority. The Palegars made use of the jungles in their areas to escape whenever the British armies tried to apprehend them. As they faced the heat from the Company forces, the Palegars indulged in looting and plundering the villages as a revenge against the government. The Palegars had great contempt for the Company officials and utter disregard for the government. When the Commissioners sent summons to them to appear in person, the replies they gave and the excuses they cited are indicative of their scant respect for the authorities.

The Chittoor Palegars' revolt also marks the conflict between the centuries –old earlier setup and modern methods in matters like land revenue, the army and every aspect of administration. Though the Palegars decided to rebel against the government, refused to surrender to the Officer commanding the forces, declined the offers of the Commissioners, they had such faith in Thomas Munro that many of them crossed over to the neighboring Cuddapah District to surrender to him.

The revolt of Gulam Rasool Khan, the Nawab of Kurnool in 1839 was a part of the larger Wahabi conspiracy that was spreading all over the country. The Wahabi movement in the Deccan was spearheaded by Mubarez-ud-Doulah and Rasool Khan, like many other Indian princes, came under its influence. Mubarez who had great access to wealth as the brother of the Nizam, and having his own private army, funded the movement in the south. With his hatred for the British, he wanted to enlist a large number of Indian chiefs who were opposed to the British rule. He sent his spies to places like Lahore, Sindh, Gwalior, Bombay, Madras, Sholapur, Kurnool etc. to enlist support from his friends there. The way these spies carried Mubarez's correspondence with utmost secrecy, is remarkable. Wearing steel bangles and rings in a particular way for identification, carrying letters concealed in turbans and in Amulets, misleading the British intelligence agents, preaching the anti- British sentiments among the sepoys in the British army, and exhorting people to rise against the British through discourses in the mosques in the garb of Moulvis - were some of the unique methods evolved by the spies employed by Mubarez as well as by the Nawab of Kurnool.

The large quantities of arms and ammunition that the Nawab of Kurnool got manufactured and stored in the secret underground vaults only speaks of the commitment he had towards the mission he undertook as a part of the Wahabi movement against the British. If the activities of Mubariz-ud-daulah were not unearthed on time by the Enquiry Commission at the behest of Gen. Fraser, the Resident at Hyderabad, the establishment of an arsenal by the Nawab of Kurnool would not have come to light. With the kind of support assured by several chiefs, it is not difficult to imagine what the consequences might be if the conspiracy was not detected.

When it came to light that the Nawab of Kurnool was in secret alliance with the Wahabis at Hyderabad under the leadership of Mubarez, the British decided at once to take action. The appointment of the Commission to enquire and the dispatch of armies from Bellary and from Hyderabad were only to crush the Nawab even before the findings of such a Commission. The attack on Rasool Khan and his defeat in the hands of the Company forces was indicative of the vengeance of the government towards the Nawab. The treatment meted out to Rasool Khan and his family after the defeat also speaks of the harsh manner in which the government wanted to put down whoever opposed its authority. Rasool Khan's spirit of sacrifice and his tragic end in captivity at Trichinopalle only made him a martyr for the cause of the anti-British feeling at least in this part of Andhra.

The Narasimha Reddy revolt in 1846 was the most daring of all the Palegars' revolts in the Ceded Districts and one of the famous in south India under the Company administration. Though the revolt was spearheaded by a single individual, there were a number of supporters of Reddy during the revolt. The unstinted help rendered by the numerous Kattubadidars is an indication of the discontent among the rural constabulary whose traditional land rights the British wanted to abolish.

The revolt of Reddy which was on the lines of Robin hood, was unique in many ways. His daring acts of violence against the symbols of government authority like the attack on the Treasury and the killing of the Thahasildar etc. evoked great admiration among the people. A large number of British army men and sepoys were also killed by Narasimha Reddy and his able followers. His courageous exploits are still remembered by the people in Rayalaseema and the great fund of folk literature prevalent in this region is a testimony to it.

Narasimha Reddy revolt had far reaching repercussions even at the Presidency level when several questions with regard to the resumption of Inams arose. The denial of the Nossum pension to Narasimha Reddy was strongly felt to be responsible for his revolt. This revolt made the government to adopt a more liberal policy towards the grants which were under long and undisputed possession.

The orders issued by the government rejecting the inheritance of Inam property by adoption unless such adoption was reported at least six months before the death of the party making it, was contested by many. The Court of Directors proposed to limit the continuance of the land grants to the lives of the existing holders. But the rebellion of Narasimha Reddy induced the government to adopt a more liberal policy with regard to the long undisputed possession. This ultimately led to the appointment of the Madras Inam Commission on 16 November, 1858 with G.N. Taylor as the Commissioner.

Immediately rules were framed which gave considerable powers to the District Collectors to continue Inams in all ordinary cases, but were to report to the Board of Revenue and the government in such cases where the Inams have passed out of the original family or passed through a female line. As Narasimha Reddy's claim to the Nossum pension was through the female line, this act of the government had added significance.

Perhaps the most representative rebellion in Andhra of the traditional chiefs and revenue collectors who lost their powers because of the colonial measures was the rebellion of the Palegars of Chittoor. The revolts of the Zamindars of Ganjam District reflected the general discontent due to the dispossession of the traditional rights of such Chiefs. The revolts both in the Northern Circars as well as in the Ceded districts were propelled by the new systems in the land revenue policies, the enhancement of Peishcush, the indiscriminate cancellation of the Inams, the abolition of the Kattubadi peons, disbanding of the traditional armies etc.

The restorative agenda of these movements revealed the inability of the peasantry to articulate their own politics where the peasants and the Kattubadidars were led by traditional elites. Therefore the pre- 1857 rebellions were both structured and limited by the imposition of the colonial measures on a feudal system. This to a large extent ensured that they remained pre-modern in both perception and deed.

# Select Bibliography


## 1. PRIMARY SOURCES

### A. *Manuscripts*

Board of Revenue Consultations

Circulars from the Zamindar's office (Huzur)

Day Books (Palace Account Books )

District Records, Cuddapah, 1802-1856.

District Records, North Arcot, 1856-1911.

District Records, Chittoor, 1911-1948.

Goshwara Account Books.

Jamabandy (Annual Settlement) Accounts.

Zamindars' Correspondence.

Manuals of Rules of the Zamindari.

Retained Disposals( R.D.s)

Title Deeds of the Khanigi Lands.

Village officers' Account Books.

### B. *Printed Documents*

1 Official Records;

*A Concise history of the Jaghirs and Palayams in the District of North Arcot, 1864- 65,* Collector's Office, Chittoor.

*Descriptive memoirs of Irrigation works in the Gudiyatham Minor Basin, Punganur and Bangarupalyam Zamindaries and Madanapalle Taluk*, (Madras,1900)

*Guide to the Records of North Arcot District, 1800-1835,* Collector's Office, Vellore.

*Hand-Book to the revenue records of the Ceded Districts,* Madras, 1932.

*Standing Order of the Board of Revenue,(Land Revenue Settlement and Miscellaneous, 1919,* Madras, 1920, in 2 Vols.

*The Chittoor District Gazettes 1911-1929, (publication of Official News*) Regional Office of the State Archives, Tirupati.

*The Fort St. George Gazette,* Weekly publication of official News.

**1. Official Reports**

*Benson's Report on the tour of Cuddapah and North Arcot District, 1878-1879*, (Madras, 1880).

C Rundall's Revenue Settlement Report of North Arcot District, 1890.

Annual Reports of on the Administration of the Madras Presidency During the years from 1860-61 to 1938-39.

*Report of the Commissioners for the Interrogation of Alleged Cases of Torture in the Madras Presidency,* Madras, 1855.

*Report on the District plan of Chittoor*, by V.S. Sampath, Chittoor Collectorate.

*District Census Hand Book: Chittoor District*, By T. Vedantam (Ed.), Hyderabad, 1973.

**2. Manuals, Gazettes and Gazetteers**

Boswell, J.A.C. *Manual of Nellore District*, Madras, 1873.

Brakenbury, C.F. *Madras District Gazetteers, Cuddapah*, Madras, 1915.

Chetty, N. Gopalakrishnama, *A Manual of Kurnool District*, Madras, 1886.

Cox, Arthur F. *A Manual of the North Arcot District,* Madras, 1881.

Gribble, J.D.B. *A Manual of the District of Cuddapah,* Madras, 1875.

Maclean, C.D. *Manual of the Administration of the Madras Presidency,* Madras, 1885-1893.

Rajagopal, M.V. "Chittoor District Gazetteer" (Draft) AP State Archives, Hyderabad, 1969.

Rice, B. Lewis, *Mysore gazetteer,* Revised. Edition, London, 1897.

Richards, F.J. *Madras District Gazetteers: Salem, Madras, 1918, 2 Vols.*

Sivasankaranarayana, Ch. *Cuddapah District Gazetteer,* Hyderabad, 1967.

Stuart, Harold A. *Madras District Manuals: North Arcot,* Madras, 1895.

*The Freedom Struggle in Hyderabad,* Vol.I, Hyderabad, 1956

*The Chronology of Modern Hyderabad,* Central Record Office by the Government, Hyderabad, 1954.

## SECONDARY SOURCES

### 1. BOOKS

Anderson, G. *British administration of India,* London, 1913.

Aitchison, C.U. *A Collection of Treaties Engagements and Sunnads,* vol.V, Calcutta,1864, Vol. IX. Calcutta, 1892.

Arbuthnot, A.J. *Selections from the Minutes and other official writings of Major –General Sir Thomas Munro,* Madras, 1886.

Archana Sharma, *The 1857 Rebellion: A Pre History,* People's Democracy, (Weekly Organ of the Communist Party of India,) Vol. XXXI, No,09, March, 04, 2007.

Aziz, S.D.V, *Gulam Rasool Khan,* Tel. Kurnool, 2011.

............ *Tharinekanti Muttadi*, Tel. Kurnool, 2008.

............ *Palegadu, Uyyalawada Narasimha Reddy*, Tel. rpt. Hyderabad, 2010.

Baden –Powell, B.H. *The Land Systems of British India,* London, 1892, 3 Vols.

Bangorey,(ed.) *Glimpses of Local History from C.P. Brown's Letters*, (Tel.) Tirupati, 1978.

Bapineedu, Maganti. *Andhra Sarvaswamu,* Rajahmundry, 1961.

Bradshaw, John. *Sir Thomas Munro and the British Settlement of the Madras Presidency,* London, 1906.

Beaglehole, T.H. *Thomas Munro and the Development of Administrative Policy in Madras 1792-1818, The Origins of Munro System*, London, 1966.

Briggs, Henry George, The Nizam, His History and Relations with the British Government, (first published 1861 )Rept. In 2 Vols. Delhi, 1985.

Coupland, R. *Britain and India*, London, rpt. 1943.

Donappa,Thoomati, *Andhra Samsthanamulu Sahithya Poshana*, Tel. Waltair, 1969.

Dutt, R.C. *The Economic History of India*, London, 8th. edn. London, 1956.

Edwardes, Michael. *Raj: The Story of the British In India*, London, 1967.

Ferminger, Walter, Kelley. *Historical Introduction to the Bengal portion of the Fifth Report,* rpt. Delhi, 1977.

Seshan, K.S.S., "Permanent Settlement in Andhra : Stage of Experimentation and Initial Hurdles," *Presidential Address, Modern History Section, A.P. History Congress* XVIII th. Session, 1994.

Sudarshan Rao, Y. *Andhra Between the Empires*, Hanumakonda, 1991.

Maddaiah, K. *Freedom Movement in Rayalaseema,* New Delhi, 2012.

Foster, William. *A Guide to the India Office Records, 1600-1858*, London, 1919, rpt. 1966.

Forrest, Denys. Tiger of Mysore, *The Life and Death of Tipu Sultan*, London, 1970.

Fraser, R.W. *British India*, London, 1896, rpt. New Delhi, 1974.

Frykenberg, Robert, Eric. Ed. *Land Tenure and Peasant in South Asia*, New Delhi, 1977.

Furnell, S.S. *The Mutiny of Vellore.*

Gleig, G.R. *The Life of Major –General Sir Thomas Munro Late governor of Madras, with extracts from letters and Private Papers,* London, 1830 rpt. 1831.

Gowda, M. Shankar Linge, *Indian Economic Census: Incidence of Land Rent in the Madras* Zamindaries, Madras, 1936.

Gopalakrishnan, S. (Ed.). *The South Indian Rebellions, (Before and After 1800)*, Chennai, 2007.

Gautam Gupta, *1857: The Uprising*

Hettne, Bjorn. *The Political Economy of Indirect Rule, Mysore 1881-1947* New Delhi, 1978.

Hussain, Yusuf, *The First Nizam: The Life and Times of Nizam-ul- Mulk Asaf Jah* I, rpt. Bombay, 1963.

Hill, S.C, *Yusuf Khan- The Rebel Commandant*, Reprint, 1987.

Iyengar, S. Sundararaja. *Land Tenures in the Madras Presidency, Students' Edition*, Madras, 1933.

Kesavanarayana, B. *Political and Social Factors in Andhra*, Vijayawada, 1976.

Khan, Mohd. Abdul Waheed (ed). *Brief History of Andhra Pradesh*, Hyderabad, 1972.

Kincaid and Parasnis. *A History of the Maratha People*, OUP, 1918-25, 3 Vols.

Kirmani, Mir Hussain Ali . *History of Tipu Sultan*, Col. Miles Trans. 1864, 2 nd. Edn. Calcutta, 1958.

Krishnaswami, P.R. Tom *Munro Sahib*, Madras, 1947.

Krishnaswami, S.Y. *Rural Problems in Madras: Monograph*, Madras, 1947.

Kumar,Dharma. *Land and Cast in South India,* Cambridge University press, 1965, rpt. 1992.

Maclean, C.D. *Manual of the Administration of the Madras Presidency.......*, Madras, 1885- 1893, in 3 Vols.

Karen Isaksen Leonard, *Locating Home: Indians Abroad.*

Mamidipudi Venkatarangaiyya, Andhralo Swatantra Samaram, Hyderabad, 1972.

Nilmani Mukherjee, *The Ryotwari System in Madras*, Calcutta, 1962.

Raghavaingar, Srinivasa. *Memorandum on the Progress of the Madras Presidency during the last forty years of British Administration,* Madras, 1892.

Prasada Rao, P.V.K. *Andhra Pradesh Samagra Charitra, (Tel),* Emesco, Vijayawada, 2007.

People's Democracy, VolXXXI, No. 9, March 4, 2007.

Panikkar, K.N. "Peasant Revolts in Malabar" in A.R. Desai (Ed), *Peasant Struggles in India.*

Ranga, N.G. *Economic Conditions of the Zamindari Ryots: The Report of the Enquiry Committee, 1933*, Bezwada, 1933.

___________*Revolutionary Peasants*, New Delhi, 1949.

Rao, C. Hayavadana, History *of Mysore*, Bangalore, 1946. 3 Vols.

Rajayyan,K. *Administration and Society in the Carnatic, 1701-1801*, Tirupati, 1966.

Rao, Narayana, K.V, *The Emergence of Andhra Pradesh,* Bombay, 1973.

Rao, P.R *History of Modern Andhra,.* New Delhi, 1978.

Rao, Raman, A.V. *Economic Development of Andhra Pradesh, 1766-1957*, Bombay, 1958.

Ramachandra Guha, *India After Gandhi.*

Rani Sarma,*Deodis of Hyderabad: A Lost Heritage.*

Ramachandra Rao, Dharani, *Kurnool Mandala Charithramu,* Tel. (1936) rept. Kurnool, 2001.

Reddi, V.M. and P. Raghunatha Rao, Andhra Under British Rule, Hyderabad, 1975.

Regani, Sarojini, *Highlights of Freedom Movement in Andhra Pradesh*, Hyderabad, 1972.

Reddi, Nallapareddi, Chandrasekhara, *Vikrama Simhapuri Mandala Sarvaswamu*, Tel. Nellore, 1963.

Reddi, P.C. *The Andhra Pradesh land Reforms*, (Ceilings on Agricultural Holdings), Act. 1973 with a Commentary, Nellore, 1975.

Row, R. Raghoonath, *A brief History of Kalahasthi in the Presidency of Madras,* Madras, 1891.

Sabyasachi Bhattacharjee( ed.) *Rethinking of 1857.*

Saheb, Meer Mohammad, *Extracts of Notes by European Travelers in the Books kept at the Palace of H.H. the Rajah Sahib C.I.E. of Punganur,* Madras, 1884.

Sastri, V. Lakshminarasimha, *Encyclopedia of the Madras Presidency and the Adjacent.*

*States*, n.p, n.d.

Sarada Raju, A. *Economic Conditions in Madras Presidency, 1800-1850*, Madras, 1941.

Seshan, K.S.S. *British Role in Rural Economy, (A Case study of Punganur Zamindari),* New Delhi, 1989.

Slater, Gilbert. *Economic Studies, Some South Indian villages*, London, 1918.

Sutherland, J. *Sketches of the Relations subsisting between the British Government in India and the* Different Native states, Calcutta, 1837.

Sudershan Rao, Y. *Andhra Between the Empires*, Hanmakonda, 1991.

Stein, Burton, Thomas *Munro: Origins of Colonial State and His Vision of Empire,* Oxford. 1989.

Subramanyam Reddy, Devireddy, *Uprising of 1857*, New Delhi, 2012.

Syeda Imam, *The Untold Charminar: Writings on Hyderabad.*

Taylor, Medows. *Tipu Sultan*: *Abridged and Annotated by Henry Martin*, London, n.d

Tharoor, Shashi. An Era of Darkness, *The British Empire in India*, New Delhi, 2916.

Vadivelu, A. The Ruling Chiefs, Nobles and Zamindars of India, Madras, 1915.

Venkatarangaiah,M (Ed.) .*The Freedom Struggle in Andhra Pradesh (Andhra),*vol I. Hyderabad, 1965.

Venkataramanaiah, Nelaturi. *Velugotivamsavali*, Tel. Madras, 1938.

Wilson, H.H. *A Glossary of Judicial and Revenue Terms...* London, 1885, Indian Edn. Delhi, 1968.

## II. Articles in Journals

Hanumatsastry, J. "Uyyalawada Narasimha Reddy", *Andhra Pradesh*, Telugu Monthly,, Director, Information and Public Relations, Hyderabad, December, 1974, pp. 40-42.

Seshan, K.S.S. "Chittoor Palegarla Viplavam 1804" (Tel) in *Andhra Pradesh*, Government of A.P. Govt. Publication, Hyderabad, March, 1978. pp. 7-11.

___________"Of Passion, Rebellion and Conspiracy," *The Hindu, Metro Plus,* 10 June, Hyderabad, p. 4.

___________"Protest Over a Procession", *The Hindu, Metro Plus*, October, 2, 2917, Hyderabad, p. 5.

Rangarajan, A. "When the Vellore Sepoys Rebelled", The Hindu, Sunday, Magazine Section, Chennai, 6 August, 20o6, p. 4.

Anjaneyulu, M.S.R. "Permanent Settlement in the Second Division of the Visakhapatnam District- A Case Study", *Itihas,* Journal of the AP State Archives, Hyderabad Vol. IV, No.2. 1976.

Azad, Melampati. "Challapalle Zamindari Bhoomula Akramana Udyamamu" *Visalandhra,* Tel. Vijayawada, Vol. 29, No. 106, 12 September, 1979.

Dua, J.C. "Poligars: Their Rise in the Ceded Districts" *Proceedings of the Indian History Congress*, 33 rd. Session, 1972.

Morris, David Moris. "Economic Change and Agriculture in Nineteenth Century India", *I.E.S.H.R,* Delhi, Vol. III, No. 2, June, 1966.

Nayeem, M.A. "Mughal Documents Relating to the Peishcush of the Zamindars of South India", *I.E.S.H.R,* Delhi, Vol. XII, No. 4, Oct-Dec. 1975.

Raghu, Y. "Tharnekal Rythanga Poratam", *Proceedings of the Andhra Pradesh History Congress,* 30th. Session, 2006.

Reddy,D. Krishna. "Naati Viprapuri, Neti Uppanelli" Tel. *Andhra Prabha*, Bangalore, 4 March, 1978.

Sarkar, Jagdish Narayan. "A Survey of Economic Conditions in India during the first half of the Eighteenth Century", *Itihas*, Hyderabad, Vol.1, No.1, Jan-July, 1973.

# Appendices

## APPENDIX - 1

### Important Centres of Resistance in India during 1763-1856

1. Sanyasi Revolts: 1763-1800; Dhaka, Rajasahi 1763, Cooch Bihar, 1766; Patna,1767; Jalpaiguri, Rangapur, 1766-60, 1771, 1776; Purnea, 1779-71, Mymensingh, 1773.
2. Midnapur, 1766-67.
3. Rajas of Dhalbhum, 1766-67.
4. Roshnarabad (Tripura), 1766-68.
5. Sandip, near Naokhali, 1769-70.
6. Moamarias, Jorhat and Rangapur, 1769-99.
7. Checkmas, Chittagong,1776-89.
8. Gorakhpur, 1781.
9. Peasants, Rangapur, 1783.
10. Birbhum and Bishnupur, 1788-89.
11. Chuar, Peasants, Midnapur; 1799.
12. Peasants, Bakargunj, 1792.
13. Vizianagaram, 1794.
14. Bednur, 1799-1800.
15. Kerala Verma, Kottayam, 1797, 1800-05.

16. Sylhet, 1787; Khasis, 1788,Agha Muhammad Reza, 1799.
17. Vazir Ali, Oudh, 1799.
18. Ganjam and Gumsur,1800,1835-37.
19. Palamau, 1800-02.
20. Polegars of Tinnevelley, Ramanathapuram, Sivaganga, Sivagiri, Madurai, 1795-1805 (North Arcot), Chittoor 1803-05.
21. Vellore Mutiny, 1806.
22. Bhivani, 1809.
23. Naiks of Bhograi,Midnapur District, 1809-10.
24. Velu Thambi of Travencore, 1808-09.
25. Chiefs of Bundelkhand, 1808-12.
26. Abdul Rehman of Surat, 1810.
27. Benaras Harthal and agitation, 1810-11.
28. Parlakimidi, in Ganjam District, 1813-34.
29. Cutch, 1815-32.
30. Rohillas of Bareilly, Philibit, Shajahanpur, Rampur, 1816.
31. Hathras, 1817.
32. Paiks of Cuttack, Khurda, Pippili, Puri, etc. 1817-18.
33. Bhills of Khandesh, Dhar, Malwa, 1817-31, 1846, 1852.
34. Kols of Singhbhum, Chotanagpur, Sambalpur, Ranchi, Hazaribagh, Palamau, Chaibasa,1820-37.
35. Mers of Merwara, 1819-21.
36. A platoon of Bengal Army, Barrackpore, 1824.
37. Gujars of Kunja, (near Roorki) 1824.
38. Sindgi, nearBijapur, 1824.
39. Bhivani, Rewari, Hissar, Rohtak, 1824-26.
40. Kalpi 1824.

41. Kittur, Belgam District, 1824-29.
42. Kolis Thana, 1828-30.
43. Ramosis of Poona, 1826-29.
44. Garos also called, Pagal Panthis revolt, Sherpur, Mymensingh Dist. 1825-27, 1832-34.
45. Gadadhar Singh, Assam, 1828-30.
46. Kumar Rupchand, Assam, 1830.
47. Khasis under Tirot Singh, 1829-33.
48. Singhphos, Assam- Burmah border, 1830-31; 1843.
49. Akas, Assam, 1829, 1835-42.
50. Wahabis, Bihar, Bengal, NWFP, Punjab, 1830-61.
51. Titu Mir, Twenty four Parganas, 1831.
52. Peasants of Mysore, 1830-31.
53. Visakhapatnam, 1830-33.
54. Bhumji, Manbhum, 1832.
55. Coorg, 1833-34.
56. Gonds, Sambalpur, 1833.
57. Naikda, Rewa Kantha, 1838.
58. Farazis, Faridpur, 1838-47.
59. Khamtas, Sadiyas, Assam, 1839.
60. Surendra Sai, Sambalpur, 1839-62.
61. Badami, 1840.
62. Bundelas, Sagar, 1842.
63. Salt Riots, Surat, 1844.
64. Gadkari, Kolhapur, 1844.
65. Savanthavadi, North Konkan Coast, 1844-47.
66. Uyyalavada Narasimha Reddy, Kurnool, 1846-47.

67. Khonds, Orissa, 1848.
68. Nagpur, 1848.
69. Garos, Garo Hills, 1846-66.
70. Abors, N.E India, 1848-1900.
71. Lushais, Lushai Hills, 1849-92.
72. Nagas, Naga Hills, 1849-78.
73. Umarzias, Bannu, 1850-52.
74. Survey Riots, Khandesh, 1852.
75. Saiyads of Hazara, 1852.
76. Nadir Khan, Rawalpindi, 1853.
77. Santhals, Rajmahal, Bhagalpur, Birbhum, 1855-56.

*Source: The 1857 Rebellion: A Pre-History,* People's Democracy, (Weekly organ of the Communist Party of India, ), Vol. XXXI, No. 09, March, 04, 2007.

## APPENDIX - II

## (Treaty by which the Ceded Districts were handed over to the East India Company)

Treaty relating to the acquisition of territories, concluded by the British with the Nizam of Hyderabad.

TREATY entered into by the Honourable British East India Company and His Highness the Nizam. Under date the 12th November, 1766.

A Treaty of perpetual honour, favour, alliance and attachment between the great Nawab, high in status, famous as the sun, Nawab Asoh Jah Nizam –Ool –Mulk, Meer Nizam Ali Khan, Bahadoor, Puttah Jung Sepoy Sirdar, and the Honourable English East India Company ; signed, sealed and ratified, on the one part by His Highness the said Nuwab, and on the other by John Calliaud,

Esquire, Brigadier –General, invested with full powers, on behalf of the said Company.

Done at Hyderabad, the 9th of the moon Jumadee- oos-Sanee, in the year of Hijree 1180, equal to 12th November, 1766.

Article 1.- The Two contracting parties do, by virtue of this treaty of honour, favour, alliance and friendship, solemnly engage a mutual assistance to esteem the enemies of one the enemies of both ; and, contrariwise, the friends of one, the friends of the other.

Article 2.- The Honourable East India Company, in return for the gracious favours received from his Highness, consisting of Sunnads for the five Circars of Ellore, Chicacole, Rajahmundry, Mustaphanuggur, and Murtezanuggur, expressing the free gift thereof on them and their heirs, forever and ever do hereby promise and engage to have a body of their troops ready to settle the affairs of his Highness government in everything that is right and proper, whenever required, provided that they be at liberty to withdraw the whole ,or such part thereof as they shall judge proper, whenever either the safety of their own settlements and possessions, or the peace and tranquility of the Carnatic be the least endangered ,( in case of their failing out, of which circumstance God forbid,) thereof to his Highness in their power.

Article 3- The Honourable East India Company do further engage and promise that in whatever year the assistance of their troops shall not be required, they will pay to his Highness as a consideration for the free gift of the above mentioned five Circars, forever and ever, the following sums, by kists, as specified in the 8th. article of this treaty, viz; for the three Circars of Rajahmundry, Ellore, and Mustaphanuggur, five lakhs of rupees, and for those of Chicacole and Murtezanuggur, as soon as they are in their hands, and the settling the same is well effected, two lakhs each, in all nine lakhs of rupees per annum.

Article 4- The reduction of the Chicacole Circar, by the blessing of God, the company will effect as soon as possible; but that of Murtezanuggur, in consideration of his Highness having by former agreements given it to his brother, Basalat Jung, as a Jagheer, the Honourable East India Company do promise and engage not to take possession of until it be his Highness's pleasure, or until the demise of his said brother; but to prevent all future disputes and difficulties that may hereafter arise concerning the same, the aforesaid Company do further explain their intentions in the following article.

Article 5- As the Circar of Murtezanuggur borders on that of Nizampatnam, and the country of the Carnatic, which, by virtue of the former and present treaties and alliances of the aforesaid Company, are bound to maintain and protect in all its extent, therefore, in case the said Basalat Jung, his agents or dependents, should cause any disturbances to the prejudice thereof, it is hereby agreed on by both parties that the aforesaid Company shall then have it in their power to take immediate possession of that Circar.

Article 6- As, by the tenor of the second article, of this treaty, the aforesaid Company have engaged to furnish a body of troops to be ready to march to the assistance of his Highness, it is agreed by both parties, that the expenses thereof shall be paid in the following manner; if the expense of the number of troops his Highness may require should fall short of the sum of five lakhs of rupees mentioned to be paid for the three Circars of Rajahmundry, Ellore and Mustaphanuggur, the Company will account to his Highness for what balance may remain due ; and in case of its exceeding the above mentioned sum, the aforesaid Company do hereby engage themselves to be answerable for the payment of the reminder. The same agreement, in like manner, to hold good for the sums stipulated to be paid for the two Circars of Chicacole and Murtezanuggur, when settled.

Article 7- In consideration of the fidelity, attachment, and services of the aforesaid Company, and the dependence, his Highness has upon them, his said Highness, out of his great favour, does hereby entirely acquit the above –mentioned Circars of all arrears and demands, down to the present date of these writings.

Article 8- In case the assistance of the Honourable Company's troops is not required, the annual stipulated sum, expressed in the third article of this treaty, the aforesaid Company do engage to pay, in three kists, after the following manner, and to give Soucar security for the same, viz: the first payment, the 31st. of March; the second, 30th of June; and the third, the 31st of October.

Article 9- Whenever his Highness goes into winter quarters, and the troops of the other Circars have leave for that purpose, those of the aforesaid Company shall have leave also to depart to their own country.

Article 10- His Highness engages to give as early notice as possible, not less than three months, of the service in which he hill require the assistance of the troops of the aforesaid Company, that they may have timely notice to make the necessary preparations, and that the number of troops sent may be sufficient for the service of them, of which the aforesaid Company are to be left the entire and sole judges; and as the success of all expeditions depends much upon secrecy in council, both parties do hereby engage themselves not to reveal any such designs as they may communicate to each other until everything on both sides is ready for execution.

Article 11- The Honourable English East India Company, in consideration of the diamond mines, with the villages appertaining thereto, having been always dependent upon his Highness's government, do hereby agree that the same shall remain in his possession now also.

Article 12- His Highness in order to convince the whole world of the great confidence and trust he reposes in the English nation, agrees and consents that the fort of Condapillee shall be entirely garrisoned by the troops of the aforesaid Company; in consideration of which the aforesaid Company do hereby agree and consent likewise that there be a Khilladeer therein on the part of his Highness, and that the usual Jagheer annexed to the Khilladeer shall be called to him.

Article 13- In virtue of this treaty of mutual favour, alliance and friendship between the two contracting parties, his Highness promises and engages to assist the aforesaid Company with his troops when required; reserving to himself the same liberty of withdrawing the whole, or any part thereof, in the same manner as is expected, for the aforesaid Company, in the second article of treaty whenever the same shall become necessary.

Article 14- In virtue of the above treaty of favour, alliance and friendship, both parties do mutually and solemnly engage to the punctual and strict observance of all and every one of the above mentioned articles, that from this time, all doubts and suspicions shall cease between them, and in their room a perpetual, just, and sincere confidence be established, so that the great affairs of the Deccan Government and the business of the Company may increase every day in honour, in riches, and in happiness, from generation to generation.

In confirmation of which, his Highness on the one part, and John Calliaud, Esquire, Brigadier – General, invested with full powers from the English Company, on the other, have hereunto affixed their hands and seals.

Dated in Hyderabad, the 9th. of moon Jumadee-oos- Sanee in the year of the Hijree 1180, equal to the 12th. of November, 1766.

*Source:* Henry George Briggs, *THE NIZAM : His History and Relations with the British Government,* Vo.II, 1861, pp. 226-230.

## APPENDIX - III

### TRANSLATION of a Sunnud under the seal of NIZAM ALEE KHAN for the five Circars

Be it known to the Deshmookes, Deshandias, Mookadums, husbandsmen, and inhabitants of the Circars of Rajahmundry, Ellore, Mustaphanuggur, Chicacole and Murtezanuggur, belonging to the Suoobahship of Hyderabad, that out of our great favour and goodness, from the 9th of moon Jamadee-00s-Sanee, in the year of Faslee, 1176, equal to the 12th. of November, 1766, the whole of the said Circars (the Jagheer of Mustaphanuggur, *alias,* Condapillee Fort, and the usual villages appertaining to the diamond mines excepted) are now given to and conferred upon the European English Company, by way of *enam,* or free gift, forever and ever agreeable to their petition, signed by us, in return for which they, the English Company, are to pay the annual sum of nine lakhs of rupees, and to stand to all Sebundy charges, and whatever earthly or heavenly mis-chances may happen. You therefore, our above mentioned Deshmookees, & c, are herby required, with contented minds, to live in obedience to the above Company's deputies, and to pay the proper revenues at the fixed and roper times.

Looking upon this as a positive order, obey it accordingly.

Dated the 9th of the moon Jamadee- oos- Sanee, in the year of the Hijree 1180, equal to the 12th of November, 1766.

*Source:* Henry George Briggs, *THE NIZAM : His History and Relations with the British Government,* Vol, .II, 1861, pp. 230-231.

## APPENDIX - IV

(The treaty by which the Northern Circars were handed over to the East India Company)

TREATY BETWEEN NIZAM AND THE BRITISH EAST INDIA COMPANY, DATED 12th. OCTOBER, 1800

TREATY OF PERPETUAL and GENERAL DEFENSIVE ALLIANCE between the Honourable East India Company and his Highness the Nuwab Nizam –Ool- Daulah Asoph Jah Bahadoor, Soobedar of the Deccan, his children, heirs, and successors; settled by Captain James Achilles Kirkpatrick, Resident at the Court of his Highness by virtue of the powers delegated to him by the Most Noble Richard Marquis Wellesley, most Honourable Privy Council, Governor-General in Council, appointed by the Honourable Court of Directors of the said Honourable Company, to direct and control all their affairs in the East Indies, and Governor-General in Council of all the British possessions in the East Indies.

Whereas, by the blessings of God, an intimate friendship and union have firmly subsisted, for a length of time, between the Honourable East India Company and his Highness the Nuwab Nizam – Ood- Daulah Asoph Jah Bahadoor, and have been cemented and strengthened by several treaties of alliance, to the mutual and manifest advantage of both powers, who, with uninterrupted harmony and concord having equally shared the fatigues and dangers of war and the blessing of peace, are, in fact, become one and the same in interest, policy, friendship, and honour. The powers aforesaid adverting to the complexion of the times, have determined on principles of precaution and foresight, and with a view to the effectual preservation of constant peace and tranquility, to enter into a general defensive alliance, for complete and reciprocal protection of their respective territories, together with those of their several allies and dependants, against the unprovoked aggression or unjust encroachments of all or of any enemies whatever.

Article 1- The peace, union and friendship so long subsisting between the two States shall be perpetual, the friends and enemies of either shall be the friends and enemies of both; and the contracting parties agree, that all the former treaties and agreements between the two states, now in force, and not contrary to the tenor of this engagement, shall be confirmed by it.

Article 2- If any power or State whatever shall commit any act of unprovoked hostility or aggression against either of the contracting parties, or against their respective dependants or allies, and after due representation shall refuse to enter into amicable explanation or shall deny the just satisfaction or indemnity which the contracting parties shall have required, then the contracting parties will proceed to concert and prosecute such further measures as the case shall appear to demand.

Article 3- For more distinct explanation of the intent and effect of this agreement, the Governor- General in Council, on behalf of the Honourable Company, hereby declares that the British Government will never permit any power or state whatever to commit with impunity any act of unprovoked hostility or aggression against the rights or territories of his Highness the Nizam, but will, at all times, maintain the same, in the same manner as the rights and territories of the Honourable Company are now maintained.

Article 3 (a)- With a view to fulfill this treaty of general defense and protection, his Highness the Nuwab Asoph Jah agrees that two battalions of sepoys, and one regiment of cavalry, with a due proportion of guns and artillery men, shall be added in perpetuity, to the present permanent subsidiary force of six battalions of sepoys, of 1000 firelocks each, and one regiment of cavalry, 500 strong (with their proportion of guns artillery men) so that the whole of the subsidiary force furnished by the Honourable East

India Company to his Highness, shall henceforth consist of eight battalions of sepoys (or 8000 firelocks) and two regiments of cavalry (or 1000 horse) with their requisite compliment of guns, European artillery men, lancers, and pioneers, fully equipped with warlike stores and ammunition; which force is to be stationed, in perpetuity, in his Highness territories.

Article 4- The pay of the above mentioned additional force shall be calculated at the rate of the pay of the existing subsidiary forces, and shall commence from the day of the entrance of the said additional force into his Highness's territories.

Article 5- For the regular payment of the whole expense of the said augmented subsidiary force (consisting of 8000 infantry, 1000 cavalry, and their usual proportion of artillery), his Highness the Nuwab Asoph Jah hereby assigns and cedes to the Honourable Company, in perpetuity, all the territories acquired by his Highness, under the treaty of Srirangapatnam on the 18th. March, 1792, and also all the territories acquired by his Highness under the treaty of Mysore, on 22nd June, 1799, according to the schedule annexed to this treaty.

Article 6- Certain of the territories ceded by the foregoing article to the Honourable Company being inconvenient, from their situation to the northward of the river Toombuddrah, his Highness the Nuwab Asoph Jah, for the purpose of rendering the boundary line of the Honourable Company's possessions a good and well defined one, agrees to retain the districts in question, namely Coul, Gujjenderghur, and other s(as marked in the annexed Schedule), in his own possession ; and, in lieu thereof assigns and cedes, in full and in perpetuity, to the Honourable Company, the districts of Adonee, together with whatever other territory his Highness may be possessed of, or is dependent on his Highness's government, to the south of the Toombuddrah, or to the south of the Krishnah, below the junction of those two rivers.

Article 7- The territories to be assigned and ceded to the Honourable Company by the fifth article, or in consequence of the exchange stipulated in the sixth article, shall be subject to the exclusive management and authority of the said Company and of their officers.

Article 8- Whereas the actual produce of a considerable portion of the districts ceded to the Honourable Company by article fifth, is ascertained and acknowledged to be greatly inferior to their nominal value, as specified in the Schedule annexed to this treaty, and the said districts cannot be expected, for a long course of years, to reach their said nominal value ; and whereas differences might hereafter arise between the contracting parties, with respect to the real value of the same, and the friendship and harmony happily subsisting between the contracting parties be disturbed by discussions relating to the adjustment of accounts of the produce and value of the said districts; in order to preclude all causes of any such future difference or discussion between the two states, the said east India Company agrees to accept the said districts (with the reservation stated in the sixth article) as a full and complete satisfaction for all demands, on account of the pay and charges to the said subsidiary force, and therefore to whatever length of time, the actual produce of the said districts shall prove inadequate to the amount of subsidy payable by the Highness, on account of the said subsidiary force, no demands shall ever be made by the Honourable Company upon the treasury of his Highness on account of any such deficiency, or on account of any failure in the revenues of the said districts, arising from unfavorable seasons, the calamity of war, or any other cause from Highness the Nizam, on his part, with the same friendly views, hereby renounces all claim to any arrears or balances which may be due to hi from the said districts, beyond the amount of the subsidy payable by his Highness, on account of the said subsidiary force, the true intention and meaning of this article being, that the cession of the said districts and the exchanges stipulated in the sixth article, shall be considered as final close and termination of accounts between the contracting parties, with respect to charges of the said subsidiary force.

Article 9- After the conclusion of this treaty, and as soon as the British Resident shall signify to his Highness Asoph Jah, that the Honourable Company's officers are reared to take charge of the Districts ceded by the fifth article, his Highness will immediately issue the necessary Purwannahs, or orders, to his officers to deliver over charge of the same to the officers of the Company; and it is hereby stipulated, and agreed that all collections made by his Highness's officers subsequent to the date of the said Purwannahs, or orders, and before the officers of the Company shall have taken charge of the said districts, shall be carried to the account of the Honourable Company.

Article 10- All forts situated within the districts to be ceded to aforesaid, shall be delivered to the officers of the Honourable Company, with the said districts ; and his highness the Nuwab Asoph Jah engages that the said forts shall be delivered to the Honourable Company as nearly as possible in the same state as that in which his Highness received them.

Article 11- His Highness the Nuwab Asoph Jah will continue to pay the subsidy of the former subsidiary force, and also that of additional troops, from his treasury, in the same manner as hitherto observed, until the Honourable East India Company's officers shall have obtained complete possession from his Highness's officers of the country ceded to the said Company by the fifth article. The Company will not claim any payments of subsidy from his Highness's treasury, after their officers shall have obtained possession of the said districts from the officers of his Highness.

Article 12- The Contracting parties will employ all practicable means of coalition to prevent the calamity of war; and for that purpose will, at all times, be ready to enter into amicable explanation s with other states, and to cultivate and improve the general relations of peace and amity with all the powers in India, according to the true spirit and tenor of this defensive treaty. But if a war should unfortunately break out between contracting parties and any other power whatever, then his Highness the Nuwab Asoph Jah engages that, with the reserve of two battalions of Sepoys, which are to remain near his Highness's person, the residue of the British subsidiary force, consisting of 6,000 infantry and 9000 horse of his Highness's own troops, making together an army of 12,000 infantry and 10,000 cavalry, with their requisite train of artillery and warlike stores of every kind, shall be immediately put in motion, for the purpose of oozing the enemy; and his Highness likewise engages to employ every further effort in his power for the purpose of bringing into field, as seedily as possible the whole force which he may be able to supply from his dominions, with a view to the effectual prosecution and seedy termination of the said war. The Honourable Company, in the same manner, engage on their art, in this case, to employ in active operations against the enemy the largest force which they may be able to furnish, over and above the said subsidiary force.

Article 13- Whenever war shall appear probable, his Highness the Nuwab Asoph Jah engages to collect as many as Banjarahs as possible, and to store as much grain as may be practicable in his frontier garrisons.

Article 14- Grain and all other articles of consumption and provisions, and all sorts of materials for wearing apparel, together with the necessary quantity of cattle, horses, and camels, required for the use of the subsidiary force, shall, in proportion to its present augmentation, be, as heretofore, entirely exempted from duties.

Article 15- As by the present treaty the union and friendship of the two states are so firmly cemented, as they may be considered as one and the same, his Highness the Nizam engages neither to commence nor to pursue in future any negotiations with any other power whatever without giving previous notice, and entering into mutual consultation with the Honourable East India Company's Government; and the Honourable Company's Government on their part hereby declare that they have no manner of concern with any of his Highness's children, relations, subjects, or servants, with respect to whom his Highness is absolute.

Article 16- As by the present treaty of general defensive alliance mutual defense and protection against all enemies are established, his Highness the Nuwab Asoph Jah consequently engages never to commit any act of hostility or aggression against any power whatever; and in the event of differences arising, whatever adjustments of tem the Company's government, weighing matters in the scale of truth and justice, may determine, shall meet with full approbation and acquiescence

Article 17- By the present treaty of general defensive alliance, the ties of the union, by the blessing of God, are drawn so close that the friends of any party will be henceforward considered as friends of the other, and the enemies of the other, it is therefore hereby agreed that if, in future, the Shorapoor, or Gudwall Zamindars, or any other subjects or dependants of his Highness's government should withhold the payment of the Cicar's just claims upon them, or excite rebellion or disturbance, the subsidiary force, or such portion thereof as may be requisite, after the reality of the offence shall be duly ascertained, shall be ready, in concert with his Highness's own troops, to reduce all such offenders to obedience. And the interests of the two States being now in every respect identified, it is further mutually agreed that if disturbances shall, at any time, break out in the districts ceded to the

Honourable Company by this treaty, his Highness the Nuwab Asoph Jah shall permit such a proportion of the subsidiary troops as may be requisite to be employed in quelling the same within the districts. If disturbances shall at any time break out in any part of his Highness's dominions contiguous to the Company's frontier,, to which it might be inconvenient to detach any proportion of the subsidiary troops, the British government, in like manner, if required by his Highness the Nuwab Asoph Jah, shall direct such proportion of the troops of the Company as may be most conveniently stationed for the purpose to assist in quelling the said disturbances within his Highness's dominions.

Article 18- Whereas, by the favour of providence, a perfect union, harmony, and concord have long and firmly subsisted between the Honourable Company, his Highness the Nuwab Asoph Jah, his Highness the Peishwa Rao Pundit Purdhan, and Raje Raghojee Bhonslah, therefore should his Highness Rao Pundit and Raja Raghojee Bhonslah or either of them, express a desire to participate in the benefits of the present defensive alliance, which is calculated to strengthen and perpetuate the foundation of general tranquility, the contracting parties will readily admit both or either of the said powers to be members of the resent alliance, on such terms and conditions as shall appear just and expedient to the contracting parties.

Article 19- The contracting articles being actuated by a sincere desire to promote and maintain general tranquility, will admit Dowlat Rao Scindia to be party to the present treaty whenever he shall satisfy the contracting parties of his disposition to cultivate the relations of peace and amity with both States, and shall give such securities for the maintenance of tranquility as shall appear to the contracting parties to be sufficient.

Article 20- This treaty, consisting of twenty articles, being this day settled by Captain James Achilles Kirkpatrick, with the Nuwab

Asoph Jah Bahadoor, Kirkpatrick has delivered one copy thereof in English and Persian, signed and sealed by himself, to the said Nuwab, who on his part has also delivered one copy of the same, duly executed by himself; and Captain Kirkpatrick, by virtue of especial authority given to him on that behalf by the most noble the Governor-General in Council, hereby declares the said treaty to be in full force from the date thereof, and engages to procure and deliver to his Highness, in the space of thirty days, a copy of the same from the Governor –General in Council, in every respect the counterpart of that executed by himself ; and on the delivery of such copy, the treaty executed by Captain Kirkpatrick shall be returned, but the additional subsidiary force specified in the third article shall be immediately required by his Highness the Nizam, and furnished by the Honourable Company, and all other articles shall be in full force from this time.

Signed, sealed and exchanged at Hyderabad, on the 12$^{th}$., October, Anno Domini 1800, or 22$^{nd}$. Jemmadee-Ool- Awul, Anno Hejirae 1215.

J.A. KIRKPATRICK,
Resident

*Source:* Henry George Briggs, *THE NIZAM : His History and Relations with the British Government,* Vol .II, 1861, pp. 279-287.

## APPENDIX -V

Treaty with the Nawab of Arcot by which Chittoor and Nellore in Andhra were acquired by the Company in 1801 after dispossessing the Nawab.

TREATY with AZEEM-OOL- DOWLAH—1801

Treaty for settling the SUCCESSION to the SOUBADARRY of the TERRITORIES of Arcot, and for vesting the ADMINISTRATION of the CIVIL and MILITARY GOVERNMENT of the CARNATIC PAYAN

GHAT in the UNITED COMPANY of MERCHANTS of England trading to the East Indies.

Whereas the several treaties which have been concluded between the United Company of merchants of England trading to the East Indies and their Highnesses heretofore Nawabs of Carnatic, have been intended to comment and identify the interests of the contracting parties ; and whereas, in conformity to the spirit of the alliance, the said Company did, by the Treaty concluded on the 12th July 1792, with the late Nawab Wolau Jah relinquish extensive pecuniary advantages, acquired by the previous Treaty of 1787 with the view and on the consideration of establishing a more adequate security for the interests of the British government in the Carnatic ; and whereas subsequent experience has proved that the intension of the contracting parties has not been fulfilled by the provisions of any of the Treaties heretofore concluded between them; and whereas the Musnud of the Soubadarry of Arcot having become vacant, the Prince Azeem-ool-Dowlah Bahadoor has been established by the English East India Company in the rank, property and possessions of his ancestors, heretofore Nawabs of Carnatic; and whereas the said Company and his Highness the said Prince, Azeem –Ool-Dowlah Bahadoor have judged it expedient that additional provisions should at this time be made for the purpose of supplying the defects of all former engagements and of establishing the connection between the said contracting parties on a permanent basis of security ,in all times to come; wherefore the following Treaty is now established and concluded by the Right Honourable Edward Clive, Governor in Council of Fort St. George, by and with the sanction and authority of His Excellence the Most Noble the Marquis Wellesley, K.., Governor General in Council of all the British possessions in the East Indies on behalf of the said United Company on the one part, and, by His Highness the Nawab Wolau Jah Ummeer-Ool-Dowlah Mada-Ool-Moolk Ummeer –Hind

Azeem-ool- Dowlah Bahadoor Showkut Jung Sippa Salar, Nawab Soubadarry of the Carnatic, on his own behalf, on the other art, for settling the succession to the Soubadarry of the territories of Arcot, and for vesting the administration of civil and military government of the Carnatic in the United Company of Merchants of England trading to the East Indies.

Article 1- The Nawab Azeem –Ool- Dowlah Bahadoor is hereby formally established in the state and rank, with the dignities dependent thereon, of his ancestors, heretofore Nawabs of the Carnatic and the possession thereof is hereby guaranteed by the Honourable East India Company to the said His Highness Azeem – Ool-Dowlah Bahadoor, who has accordingly succeeded to the Soubadarry of the territories of Arcot.

Article 2- Such parts of the Treaties heretofore concluded between the said East India Company and their Highnesses, heretofore Nawabs of the Carnatic, as are calculated to strengthen the alliance, to cement the friendship, and to identify the interests of the contracting parties, are hereby renewed and confirmed, and accordingly the friends or enemies of either are the friends or enemies of both parties.

Article 3- The Honourable Company hereby charges itself with the maintenance and support of the military force necessary for the defense of the Carnatic, and for protection of the rights, person, and property of the said Nawab Azeem –Ool- Dowlah Bahadoor; and with the view of reviving the fundamental principles of the alliance between his ancestors and the English nation, the said Nawab Azeem-Ool- Dowlah stipulated and agrees that he will not enter upon any negotiation or correspondence with any European or native power, without the knowledge and consent of the said English Company.

Article 4- It is hereby stipulated and agreed that the sole and exclusive administration of the civil and military governments of all the territories and dependencies of the Carnatic Payan Ghat, together with the full and exclusive right to the revenues thereof (with the exception of such portion of the said revenues as shall be appropriated for the maintenances of the said Nawab and for the support of his dignity) shall be forever vested in the said English Company; and the said Company shall accordingly possess the sole power and authority of constituting and appointing without any interference on the art of the said Nawab, all officers for the collection of the revenues, and of establishing courts for the administration of civil and criminal judicature.

Article 5- It is hereby stipulated and agreed that one-fifth art of the net revenues of the Carnatic shall be annually allotted for the maintenance and support of the said Nawab and of his own immediate family; including the Mahal of His late Highness, the Ummeer-ool- Omrah. The said fifth part shall be paid by the Company, in monthly instalments of the twelve thousand Star Pagodas; and whatever circumstances may occur, affecting the net revenues of the Carnatic, the said instalments shall not be less than twelve thousand Star Pagodas . Whatever balance of the said fifth part remain due at the at the expiration of each year shall be liquidated upon the settlement of accounts, and the said fifth part shall be at the free disposal of the said Nawab, consistently with the principles of the said alliance.

Article 6- The fifth part of the revenues, as stated in the preceding Article, shall be calculated and determined in the following manner, viz.' all charges of every description incurred in the collection of the revenues, the amount of the Jaghire lands, stated in the ninth Article in the Treaty of 1787 at Star Pagodas 2,13,421, and the sum of Pagodas 6,2,105, appropriable to the liquidation of the debts of the late Mohammad Ali, shall in the first instance, be deducted from the revenues of the Carnatic; and after the deduction of those three items, shall have been made, one fifth part of the remaining net revenue (including the Polygar

Peishcush which shall always be calculated at the sum of 2,64,704 Star Pagodas 20 Fanams 26Cash, according to the Treaty of 1792) shall be allotted for the maintenance of the said Nawab, and for the support of His Highness's dignity.

Article 7- Whereas it was stipulated by the fourth Article of the Treaty of 1792 that the sum of six lakhs twenty one thousand one hundred and five Star Pagodas should annually be applied to the discharge of certain registered debts due by the late Nawab Mohammad Ali to his private creditors, under agreements concluded between his Highness and the Honourable Company, and guaranteed by the Parliament of Great Britain, until the said registered debt should be liquidated; the Honourable English Company, accordingly hereby charges itself with the annual payment of 6,21,105 Pagodas from the revenues of the Carnatic, until the reminder of the said registered debt shall be liquidated.

Article 8- Whereas certain debts are due to the said Company by the ancestors of the said Nawab, and whereas it is expedient, in order that the present Treaty may include complete arrangement of all affairs depending between the said Company and the said Nawab, that an adjustment should be made of the aforementioned debts, wherefore the said Nawab formally and explicitly acknowledges the debt, commonly called the Cavalry loan, amounting, with its interest, to 13,24,342 Star Pagodas 6 Fanams 47 Cash, and also the portion of the registered debt heretofore paid by the Company to the creditors of the late Nawab, Wolau Jah (according to the annexed schedule) to be just debts; and whereas exclusively of the above mentioned debts, other unadjusted debts also remain, which were referred to the adjustment and decision of the Governor- General in Council of Bengal ; and whereas the said unadjusted debts have not been determined according to that intention, the said Nawab hereby engages that whenever the said determination shall be made, His Highness will acknowledge to be a just debt the amount of the balance which shall be so declared to be due to the Company. It is not however the intension of this Article to cause any diminution from the fifth part payable to the said Nawab, but, on the contrary, it is specified that no deduction shall be made from the revenue, on any account whatever, excepting the three items stated in the sixth Article, previously to the determination of His Highness proportion.

Article 9- The English Company engages to take into consideration the actual situation of the families of their Highnesses the late Nawab Wolau Jah and Omdet-Ool- Omrah Bahadoor, as well as the situation of the principal officers of His late Highness's government ; and the British government shall charge itself with the expense (chargeable on the revenues of the Carnatic) of a suitable provision for their respective maintenance. The amount of the above mentioned expenses, to be defrayed by the Company, shall be distributed, with the knowledge of the said Nawab, in such manner as shall be judged proper.

Article 10- The said Nawab Azeem –Ool- Dowlah Bahadoor shall, in all places, on all occasions, and all times, be treated with respect and attention due to His Highness's rank and situation, as an ally of the British government, and a suitable guard shall be appointed from the Company's troops for the protection of His Highness's person and place.

Article 11- The entire defense of the Carnatic against foreign enemies, and the maintenance of the internal tranquility and police of the country, having been hereby transferred to the British government, His said Highness engages not to entertain or employ in his service any armed men without the consent of the British government, who will fix, in concert with His Highness, the number of armed men necessary to be retained for purposes of state. Such armed men as His Highness may, in consequence of this Article, engage in his service, shall be paid at the exclusive cost and charge of the said Nawab.

Article 12- The Honourable East India Company shall, in conformity to the stipulations of this treaty, enter upon the exclusive administration of the civil and military government of the Carnatic, on 31st day of July, 1801; and His said Highness the Nawab shall issue orders to all his civil and military officers, to transfer the district or districts under their respective charge to such persons as shall be appointed by the said Company to manage the said districts, and also to deliver to the persons appointed, all records and official papers belonging to their respective cutcheries or offices.

This Treaty, bearing date the 31st. day of July Anno Domini 1801, and consisting of twelve Articles, having been executed by Edward, Lord Clive, Governor-in- Council aforesaid, on the one art, and His Highness Azeem- Ool- Dowlah Bahadoor on the other part, is hereby mutually interchanged, the said Edward, Lord Clive engaging that a copy of the said Treaty shall be transmitted to Fort William, for the purpose of being ratified by His Excellency the Most Noble the Marquis Wellesley, K.P., the Governor –General in Council, and that, as soon as the ratified Treaty shall be received form Bengal, it shall be delivered to His said Highness, who will then return to His Lordship the copy which he now receives.

( Sd,) CLIVE
" J.STUART
" WILLIAM PETRIE
" E.W. FOLLOWFIELD

By the Right Honourable the Governor General in Council.

(Sd.) J. WEBBE

Chief Secretary to Government

*Source:* C.U. Aitcheson, *A Collection of Treaties, Engagements & Sannads Relating to India and Neighboring Countries*, Calcutta, 1864, Vol. X, pp. 57-61.

# Index

**N**

**O**



**P**

### Q



### R